THE CROSSING

Searching for My Baltic German Ancestry
and Discovering Latvia

By Charlie Maddaus

Copyright © 2020 Charlie Maddaus

All rights reserved. No part(s) of this book may be reproduced, distributed or transmitted in any form, or by any means, or stored in a database or retrieval systems without prior expressed written permission of the author of this book.

ISBN: 978-1-5356-1743-7

Contents

Acknowledgements 5
Preface 7
Introduction 9
    Chapter One: Augusta Rathminder Maddaus: The Crossing 15
    Chapter Two: Aunt Freida 21
    Chapter Three: Maddaus Family History - What We Did Know ..27
    Chapter Four: A Flat World...33
    Chapter Five: Latvia - July 2005 37
    Chapter Six: The Road to Vecpiebalga 41
    Chapter Seven: Paistu, Estonia...47
    Chapter Eight: Return from Latvia..51
    Chapter Nine: Back to Latvia - August 2009 55
    Chapter Ten: Johann Karl Ludwig Maddaus (1820-1878) 69
    Chapter Eleven: The Artwork of Johann Karl Ludwig Maddaus ...75
    Chapter Twelve: Latvia - February 2010 101
    Chapter Thirteen: Andžs Rātminders (1805-1887).......................105
    Chapter Fourteen: Riga/Hamburg - Summer 2010......................111
    Chapter Fifteen: Jānis Rātminders (1812-1880) 117
    Chapter Sixteen: Līgo and Jāņi Midsummer Holidays - 2011 123
    Chapter Seventeen: Latvian Literature..133
    Chapter Eighteen: Latvian Relatives! 145
    Chapter Nineteen: The Life of the Village, Life of the Quest 163
    Chapter Twenty: Oscar Wilhelm Maddaus (1845-1896)..............171
    Chapter Twenty-One: Latvian Music..179
    Chapter Twenty-Two: Latvia 100 A Year of Celebration, 2018....189
Appendix 193
    Johann Karl Ludwig Maddaus Family..193
    Johann Rathminder Family (Jānis Rātminders) 195
Resources 197
About the Author 201

Acknowledgements

The pivotal point for the research for this text was my receiving an award of a Barlow Fund Travel Grant for Bates College Alumni by the Barlow Endowment for Study Abroad. Though the study I undertook was at Cambridge University in England, the travel there was the impetus to continue on to Latvia and so my search began. I owe a debt of gratitude to the Barlow Fund.

The writing began as a function of my enrollment in the Maine Writing Project, the initial course for my M. Ed. in Secondary Literacy at the University of Maine at Orono. Thanks to instructors Cindy Dean, Rich Kent, Dave Boardman, and Ken Martin for their encouragement and/or feedback and all the other Literacy instructors who guided me through the program.

Completing the program would probably not have been possible without my brother John and his association with the University of Maine, as well as the spare room he offered so many times when I had evening classes at the university. John also got the family history ball rolling, so to speak, with his research of our family tree back in the early 1990s which uncovered the first of two Johann Maddaus paintings in Latvia.

Eileen Marcil, our 4th cousin from Quebec, filled in some of the Hamburg history related to Johann Maddaus and his sister, her ancestor Johanne Maddaus Winterhof.

Certainly, my parents played a part in this. My father, Ingo, Jr., while not the least bit interested in family history, gave me a taste of travel with trips to Baxter State Park, Alaska and the Pacific Northwest. And my mother, Elsie, who just turned 100, is the supreme example of the librarian who leaves no stone unturned in researching a subject. The travel and the research are a function of the examples they set in my upbringing.

To Beth, who has made so many trips to Latvia with me and seemed to enjoy it as much as I do, and has stayed home an almost equal number of times when I have the urge to make one more, I owe so much. Her edit of this text has saved me a tremendous amount of time and stress and her encouragement has been priceless.

To my sons Caleb and Jacob, this is for you, so you know where we come from. And for your sister Kate, who is no longer with us but in spirit. Her memory is a part of everything I do, this text included.

Preface

The following is an attempt to outline the discovery of my Maddaus/Rathminder/Rātminders family history in what is now present-day Latvia.

Ancestors are depicted mostly through the historical records they are represented in and the artistic work they have left behind. Latvian relatives have been gracious in sharing their lives and family experiences. I hope I have presented them accurately.

Because this covers the early 19th Century through the present, I've stumbled at times with the transitions in language used to record the history of the period. German church record, Russification, the early Latvian written text, modern Latvian and my own limited skills beyond the English language have made some of what follows somewhat confusing at times. Jahn Rathminder at his birth, is later Johann Rathminder and now referred to as Jānis Rātminders in his native Latvian. I've fractured some of the Latvian names with an English spelling so I apologize for any mistakes of that nature.

Latvia's complicated history has been difficult for many to sort out and I'm certainly no expert. I've done my best to place our ancestors within the historical times they lived, but acknowledge that I may not entirely understand them.

I offer no apologies for my love and admiration of Latvian culture and custom; Latvian's love of nature, Latvian music, Latvian literature and Latvian art has emanated from the Baltic littoral over the centuries and has sustained Latvian society to this day. Without it, Latvia would not exist. And I would not have been so enriched.

Introduction

I really cannot pinpoint the moment I decided to research my ancestry, visit some of the places associated with our family's past history, or study the cultural background we rose from. And maybe it is not important to identify that specific point in time. As with many things in life, it developed over time, from nothingness, into a life of its own.

The same goes for the decision to write this down. I guess I knew from early in my research that I would try to record what I found for posterity's sake, even before I knew the extent of what my research would entail. Like many things, the research and the writing have taken many turns along the way, so that what I initially thought I was writing this for has changed dramatically more than once, as the research has unveiled new and fascinating and sometimes tangential information.

I had, at one point, a great quotation that I have since lost, that, in effect, said that you cannot truly appreciate a writer's work unless you know where he or she is coming from. I think it was a Hemingway quote, but I am not sure. If you know the quote I am talking about, let me know, but it was probably Hemingway. He had a great many things to say about writing and writers that were elucidating, in spite of his claim that he never wanted to write about writing.

There is even a really great book called "Ernest Hemingway on Writing," edited by Larry W. Phillips, which is full of great Hemingway quotes on writing. Like

> Then there is the other secret. There isn't any symbolysm (sic). The sea is the sea. The old man is an old man. The boy is a boy and the fish is a fish. The shark are all sharks no better no worse. All

the symbolism that people say is shit. What goes beyond is what you see beyond when you know.

That is one of my favorites. So is the one quotation I cannot think of.

My point of mentioning the quotation that I have forgotten, is that knowing where a writer is coming from is similar to knowing where you are coming from. Just as knowing a writer's history and background helps to illuminate their writing, so does knowing your own personal history and background help illuminate who you are. And knowing who you are, including the part of you that predates your memory and/or birth, is essential to your journey into the future. Because otherwise the journey is not what you think it is, and not what it could be, without that additional knowledge. You cannot fully appreciate where you are going without knowing where you come from. Certainly, this is part and parcel to the growing desire in recent years for people to research their ancestry in the many online websites dedicated to just that. Ancestry.com, 23 and Me and CRI Genetics are all exploding with demand for DNA testing and family tree websites have risen in popularity as a result.

And as to Hemingway's symbolism quote, the last line applies here, too. Each time I think I know something about our past ancestry, I see the "beyond" and imagine the beyond, until I know something more.

Of course, we cannot know all of our past, or the past lives of our many ancestors. And certainly, we all have different memories and knowledge of our family history. For many people, knowing family history can be irrelevant information, or is a source of pride, or is haunting in ways we would rather not tell. The characteristics of family history vary every bit as much as the stories that arise from them and I suppose it is the variety which makes these stories interesting and important and enriching.

I recently read a book about sheep in the Lake District of Northern England that had an awful lot of information about sheep. It reminded me a lot of the cytology in Moby Dick. But beyond this bovine treasure trove of information was the story of the families who have raised sheep continuously in this region for centuries.

The book is called "The Shepherd's Life: A Tale of the Lake District," by James Rebanks. In it, Rebanks relates his grandfather's impact on him as a boy:

> We are, I guess, all of us, built out of stories. He told stories of his grandfather on his mother's side of the family, T. G. Holiday. From what I could gather, my granddad had worshipped and copied his grandfather much as I did mine. So even though I'd never met this man and he died long before I was born, there was a connection and continuity between us. My grandfather built himself up out of stories about T. G. Holiday and I built myself up out of stories of him. (70)

Reflecting on Rebanks' reverence for his grandfather and great, great grandfather, it occurred to me I did not have the connection or continuity with my ancestors that he spoke so eloquently of. As a boy, I barely knew my paternal grandfather. He visited infrequently, barely talked with me—I would give him the benefit of the doubt here, as he had four grandsons at this point—and died when I was seven years of age. My maternal grandfather died when my mother was only 3, and nearly 30 years before I was born.

So, what were the stories of our family? And who passed them along? *And what was I built up out of?* Our family stories were few and far between as though the great canvas of our family history had a few small colorless images on a blank expanse of white.

My father filled in few of the images. He seemed less interested in family history than both his devotion to teaching college mathematics and his desire to see certain far-flung sections of the American Wilderness. He spoke little of his parents, respectfully of his aunts and uncles, reverently of his two grandmothers—both of whom had the first name Augusta—and grandfathers and other ancestors were never mentioned. I do not hold this against him in any sense, by the way, as he was who he was and I learned after he was gone the reasons for some of the unspoken factors that limited our family sense of the past.

During the few times my grandparents visited in my youth, my father was most concerned with his duty to make them comfortable—including stocking the right beer for my grandfather—and I knew at a young age the relationship between son and father was not very warm. Granddad was a Wall Street businessman, an importer of German machinery, and when a war or a depression was not going on, he was apparently very good at what he did. He and my grandmother would arrive by train—The Twentieth Century Limited or the Lake Shore Express—from New York and stay at most a night or two and leave again on one of the eponymous NY Central Railroad lines. In my memory, he barely talked to me and being a shy child, I was probably somewhat intimidated by him.

The family stories were based on loose comments about the artist from Hamburg, Germany with the lyrical name—Johann Karl Ludwig Maddaus—and my father's love for his 'German Grandmother'—he would always say he had two wonderful grandmothers, one of which was Augusta Rathminder Maddaus. And it was these fine strings of family history that formed my conscious sense of ethnicity and culture for many years, well into adulthood.

So it was that desire to fill out the canvas of our family historical portrait, so to speak, that got me started and I had limited expectations at first. Visiting Latvia, the present-day country of my great grandmother Augusta's birth—it was part of the Russian Empire when she and my great grandfather emigrated to the US—and perhaps Hamburg, Germany, were the initial steps, but I was told not to expect to find any tangible evidence of our ancestors, as the war—World War II—had destroyed most all records. And my great grandmother's 'old maid' sisters had not survived the war.

I hoped to see a couple examples of Johann Karl Ludwig Maddaus art, walk the cities and towns of my ancestors and return home with the mission accomplished. If that was all I found, the story would have been written 10 years ago and ended on page 5 or page 6, with little else to add. Except for the family tree, if it could be reconstituted. I will include that and some other details in the appendix.

Speaking of the appendix, I'm reminded of what a great language English is. I love the episode on the TV series M.A.S.H. when Hawkeye Pierce is asked to perform an appendectomy on a soldier and he cracks, "Great! I wrote the book on the appendix. I wrote the appendix, too, but they took it out." What other language uses the same word for a useless body part and extraneous information in a book?

Language, of course, or multiple languages have posed some interesting obstacles in this endeavor, but not as daunting as I first expected. My English and a couple of digital translators have facilitated much of my research and the fact that most Latvians under the age of 40 or so have studied English, really has made this easier than it might have been.

With one visit to Latvia under my belt and less difficulty with the language barrier than I expected, I found that not all records were destroyed during the war and there was, indeed, more to the story than previously told. Now, after 12 visits to Latvia, I can tell what I believe is a marvelous tale of family, place and culture, far beyond my original comprehension. The canvas has become not just a finely decorated tapestry, but goes beyond the two dimensions of visual art, to encompass the spirit and soul of a culture I had not expected to experience, and I had not been prepared to experience.

To use James Rebanks' terminology, I have built this book out of the stories of our ancestors, the stories of the relatives of Augusta Rathminder Maddaus whose descendants live in Latvia today, and the stories of a vibrant culture that is called Latvian. The story is not finished but here is what I have to share so far. I hope you enjoy it.

Charlie Maddaus
October 2019

Chapter One

Augusta Rathminder Maddaus: The Crossing

Augusta Rathminder Maddaus' Lincoln Rocker

One of the few heirlooms that remains to document my father's paternal grandmother is a Lincoln rocker which sits in our living room. Dad gave it to me shortly after my first marriage. My children were all nursed and rocked in it. I do not remember whether I asked for it or he offered it but the conversation certainly began with his recollection of his two grandmothers, both named Augusta. "I had the best grandmothers," he recalled with great affection. Augusta Dorothea, his German grandmother, was the owner of the rocker, and a profound influence on her grandson in spite of her limited English and his limited German language skills. He was equally fond of his maternal grandmother, Augusta Lillian Willis Meade, but spoke more of Augusta Dorothea.

Augusta Dorothea Rathminder Maddaus, c. 1880 in Riga at age 30

The rocker is an un-upholstered version of the chair Lincoln popularized during his Presidency and which flourished in the 1860s and 1870s. Rocking chairs were especially popular in the latter part of the 19th century in America and this caned model was Augusta's favorite point of repose. Mahogany-colored and lacking the decorative arm-loops or engraved headboards, Augusta's is utilitarian, if not ornate.

This heirloom, an artifact really, is one of a very few that documents the long and satisfying life of Augusta Dorothea Rathminder Maddaus. That we have so little to remember her by seems, in itself, incongruous. Dad loved to talk about his grandmothers, to the exclusion of his parents and most other relatives. He had an abiding reverence for Augusta Dorothea and the life she lived. His passing in May 2005 erased the memory, and we are left with the chair, two photos and a few details that enable us to reconstruct her life.

Augusta was born in Riga, the capital of the Baltic Republic of Latvia, on September 12, 1850. The territory now known as Latvia, referred to as Livonia, Lettland and/or names relating to the various Baltic tribes who lived there for centuries, had been incorporated into the Russian Empire. It was ruled by Tsar Nicholas I at the time of her birth and later Tsar Alexander II who, in 1861, eliminated serfdom in the Empire, a liberal act that certainly coincided with the national movement of ethnic Latvians. Augusta's Riga, though ruled by Russia and inhabited by Latvians, was composed in part by an enclave of German merchants, as were many Baltic cities in what was referred to the Hanseatic League. Augusta spoke German all her life and immersed herself in German culture. Her selection of names of two of her children, Ingo and Freida, trace directly to her love of the historical romance novels of Gustav Freytag.

Augusta's parentage was somewhat of a mystery from what I could gather from my father. We had a short manuscript (more a one-page set of notes, really) which survived her, written in Latvian, and it suggested her father was Andžs Rathminder, who for over 60 years was teacher in the Latvian village of Vecpiebalga, 130 kilometers or so east of Riga. A school teacher of high regard, longevity and influence in Latvian culture, Andžs is included in the "Latvian Encyclopedia," published by Arveds Svabe in the 1950s.

It is known that Augusta left Riga in the mid-1870s and traveled to New York City (specifically Brooklyn) to marry Oscar W. Maddaus, the son of respected Riga portrait artist and art teacher Johann Karl Ludwig Maddaus. Oscar's emigration to the US preceded Augusta by a number of years and his marriage to her was his second. His first wife Margaret, and three children Adelaide, Clara and Oscar were apparently victims of an influenza epidemic late in 1872 into 1873. All four were interred in the Green Wood Cemetery in Brooklyn in August of 1873, in what would become the family plot.

Documentation of Augusta's initial arrival in America is not extant but it is clear she traveled from Riga with the express intent to marry

Oscar, and by May of 1877 their first of seven children, Elsa, was born. Oscar worked, at the time, as a woodcut artist and had contracts with a number of companies including The India Rubber Comb Company in College Point NY, the Remington Sewing Machine Company and Reed & Barton Flatware Company. In fact, his work for Reed & Barton may have been pivotal, as their discontent with his turn-around times and his inability to produce acceptable human figures for work on their 1877 catalog, suggests a difficult period for his business. Whether it was his work or his father's health (Johann retired his teaching position in July 1877) they returned to Riga and by May of 1878 their second child and first son, Oscar, was born there. Oscar W. and Augusta would have been in Riga on his father's death, August 1, 1878.

Four children followed during their residence in Riga—our grandfather Ingo, Freida, Senta and Harold--nearly one a year through 1883 and, while it is unclear as to when, Oscar returned to his work in Brooklyn ahead of his family. What followed had to be at once a typical event in terms of trans-Atlantic immigration, and yet a heroic effort on the part of Augusta Dorothea Rathminder Maddaus.

Armed with a US Entry Visa in her name, dated October 22/Nov. 3, 1882 and executed in the Russian capital of St. Petersburg, with her six children's name and birthdates listed (Harold added after his birth in 1883), Augusta traveled with her children and no other family members via Hamburg, Germany and Le Harve, France to New York City. All are included in the passenger list of the steamship Lessing, of the Hamburg-America Line. Built in 1874, the Lessing made frequent trips between New York and Hamburg from 1875 to 1888.

Augusta arrived with her 6 children, infant to age 6, at Castle Garden in The Battery, the very southern tip of Manhattan, on October 16, 1883, the receiving point for over 10 million immigrants between 1830 and the opening of Ellis Island in 1892. Her determination and fortitude in crossing the Atlantic with 6 children in tow, is a testament to the reverence our family holds for her. She settled in Brooklyn, surrounded by her family whom she lived with through Oscar's death in

1896 and to her own passing in 1937.

Augusta's Lincoln Rocker will forever memorialize her crossing and one family's foothold in America. That we knew so little about her and her origins is a family enigma that extended in to the 21st century.

Chapter Two

Aunt Freida

"Reee-guh," she exaggerated the first syllable of her birth-place. "Reee-guh."

Freida Maddaus, my father's Aunt Freida, was a frequent visitor in our household when I was growing up in the 1950s and 60s. She would join us for the holidays, a tradition that began with her tagging along with my grandparents, according to my older brother, but continued even after her brother Ingo, Sr., our grandfather, died in 1958. I wasn't sure of it, but I always felt that Aunt Freida's sense of family was a factor, she was close to her mother and all 5 siblings and took it upon herself to perpetuate that sense of family in her visits to her favorite nephew and his family.

Freida Maddaus on Maddaus Family vacation in Wells, Maine, 1963

Freida often joined us during our summer vacations, too, usually the last two weeks in August, right after my father's summer school teaching duties ended, but before school started up for us all in the fall. We would get settled in our modest vacation house or cottage, and three or four days later, Freida would arrive, usually by train, to join us for the balance of the vacation. She loved the life of a tourist, although I am not sure she traveled much by herself, she seemed to enjoy our vacations with us.

At the very least, she was an attraction for us 4 boys, and she was always entertaining in a reserved sort of way. After all, at age 10, I was active, inquisitive, and impressionable and Aunt Freida was 80, though she could pass for much younger. (One family story involves one of my father's first jobs as a factor in the garment industry--Freida worked in the secretarial pool and tried to pass dad off as her cousin.) She didn't hesitate to walk the beach with us, engage in card or board games or, when vacationing in Vermont, ride the single chairlift to the top of Stowe Ski Area on Mount Mansfield.

'Reee-guh' was Freida's birthplace, along with 4 of her 5 siblings, my grandfather included. One summer vacation day she told me all she knew about 'Reee-guh': that her Mumma and Daddy moved from there in the 1880's to settle in Brooklyn, NY and that it was part of Russia, or more accurately, the Russian Empire, which was ruled by the Tsar. As this was 1961, she corrected herself, stating that now Russia was the USSR. Well, I knew about the Union of Soviet Socialist Republics from school. They, or it, I was not sure, were/was the reason we had air-raid drills and hid under our desks to practice for when the Russians dropped atomic bombs on us. By age 10, I already had known for a few years how ridiculous this was—no flimsy desk would protect us from these bombs, no matter what exactly they were. The threat was real, however, and I was convinced I would never see adulthood, and later during the Vietnam War, I would never see the age of 30. Having children of my own finally put that dread to rest, replaced with the worries of parenting.

When asked to spell Reee-guh, Freida wrote RIGA in big letters. My immediate impression was that this was RI-guh with a long "i" sound, but I did not say anything because I figured Aunt Freida did not have the benefit of the advanced phonics education I did. I also questioned what Germans were doing in Russia--after all, the Maddaus family was German. Freida explained that many German people, merchants and artisans, settled there and were generally welcomed by the Tsar. The Tsar, Russia, the Soviets—all these were scary to me, and the fact that our ancestors lived among them seemed odd, that they left for America, fitting.

Aunt Freida even taught me a few lines of German, "Guten Morgen," ("Good Morning") etc., most of which I quickly forgot. I knew that Freida's mother Augusta, my great-grandmother, spoke mostly German, my grandfather and Aunt Frieda were bi-lingual (he conducted much of his import business in German), and that my father hated the language. Maybe hate is too strong a word, but Dad resisted any identification with his German ethnicity, choosing to be wholly American. He was born in 1909, lived through both World Wars having endured (or denied) his German blood with great reticence. Besides, his mother was from an English-speaking American family and he could take solace in this connection and his interest in the wholly American games of baseball and football. Dad earned his BA in mathematics at Columbia University in spite of failing German class at least once and only passing the foreign language requirement in "Technical German."

One event during a summer vacation on Lake Champlain crystalized the prevailing attitudes of my Father and his Aunt Freida. We traveled north up Lake Champlain to where it drains into the Richelieu River and then up the Richelieu to its mouth at Sorel, Quebec, on the St. Lawrence River. Knowing the U.S. Border agents would ask the identities of everyone in the car on our return, Dad explained to Aunt Freida that it might be best to say she was born in Brooklyn, rather than Riga, so as not to attract attention to our ethnicity. Identifying with either the Soviet Union, or Russia, or Germany, for that matter, was beyond his comfort zone. I never knew him to be dishonest with anyone, but this was one deception he was adamant about. Aunt Freida, on the other hand had a sort of naiveté about her identity. She was proud to be from Brooklyn, yet wanted to be honest with the authorities. Dad prevailed, speaking for everyone in the car, and the border guard was further convinced when she spoke in her heavy Brooklyn accent.

In addition to Ingo, Sr., our grandfather, Dad's Aunt Freida had 4 siblings, Elsa, Oscar, Senta and Harold. Technically, there was one other, also named Harold, who died as an infant. Elsa, the eldest, was born in Brooklyn in 1877 after Augusta came to America to marry Oscar W. Maddaus. (Oscar W.'s first wife and their three children all died in an influenza epidemic 4 or 5 years earlier.) Oscar W. and Augusta moved back to Riga where Oscar (1878), Ingo (1879), Senta (1880), Freida (1881) and the first Harold (1883) were born.

Augusta and Oscar W. made their final move to Brooklyn in 1883 and Harold (the second) was born in Brooklyn in 1890. The family grew quickly until tragedy struck with Oscar W.'s death in 1896. The six youngsters in the household went to work to support the family, as Augusta never worked outside the home. And they stayed together. Oscar and Ingo were the only ones to marry, the others choosing to live with their mother until her death in 1937.

A few anecdotes of the close-knit nature of this family survived. One involved Oscar's desire to attend the Seminary at Brown University, but lacking the resources to pay for his tuition and expenses. Ingo, then in his early years as an importer, funded his brother's attendance in the program. Uncle Oscar was to be the pastor of the Manhasset Community Church for many years, a highly regarded member of the community, charter member of the American Civil Liberties Union and frequent speaker and Reformed Church representative at ecumenical events.

When the economic downturn of 1929 turned into the Great Depression, my father observed that his father spent an entire decade without work or any visible means of support. The import/export business had dried up and he lost their house in Great Neck to foreclosure.

While it was never mentioned in the family, it is apparent that my grandparents survived those lean years as a result of the family repaying the debt. Later, my father, with a wife and young sons, would occasionally depend on the family support his father had extended, in borrowing from his Uncle Oscar, who was more than willing to help.

My memory of my grandfather was limited by the fact that he died when I was seven years old. My single image, beyond the many photos of him, is Grandpa sitting in the biggest chair in our living room, being waited on by my mother, on one of my grandparent's holiday visits. He's enjoying a glass of beer and surveying our house and family, the patriarch of the Maddaus family. Meanwhile, my father keeps up his guard for the criticism he knows will come his way.

While he never verbalized it, Dad could not hide the discomfort he felt in his father's presence. He went about taking care of his family, my brothers and I, and otherwise was the dutiful son. Dad enjoyed his Uncle Oscar more, I think, although visits to see Oscar and Hedwig, Oscar's wife, were characterized by one-part enjoyment, one-part duty. The latter was demonstrated one year on the anniversary of Oscar, Jr.'s death: Dad, my brother Philip and I had a subdued visit with Oscar and Hedwig at their retirement home, an hour away in Upstate New York. (Phil and I were cautioned to not ask to hear the old Regina disc player, usually an attraction in itself.) In spite of the somber occasion, we all knew how much they appreciated Dad's presence on such a mournful day.

In many respects, it was Aunt Freida who was the most memorable of her generation and she always seemed to me to be the free spirit in the family. She worked a number of clerical jobs, but had no definite profession, unlike her sisters Elsa who was a dental assistant and Senta who taught school. Her longevity was based on the stability of her family and a 'live and let-live' attitude. Her later years were marked by the fact that she outlived her siblings and she became disoriented to the point that my father, her closest relative, had to bring her to upstate from Brooklyn to live. As she became even older, she would wander away from home and eventually dementia set in. In her final years, she was confined to a nursing home and gradually lost her use of the English language, speaking German, the language of her mother, exclusively.

Chapter Three

Maddaus Family History
What We Did Know

With the memory of Aunt Freida's 'Reee-guh' firmly placed in my grey matter, it seemed inevitable that I would follow that prompt to search for the family's roots in Riga. A great sense of geography, a keen affinity to maps and an interest in history would, on occasion, point me towards a greater understanding of the land of our ancestors, behind the Iron Curtain in what was referred to the Latvian S. S. R.

I had one occasion to visit Europe in my younger years, involving a 1970 trip to attend a ski racing training camp in the French Alps. I was an avid skier by that point and wanted to improve my modest skills in downhill/alpine ski racing. The camp was run by Adrien Duvillard, a former French Ski Team star and included ski legends Guy Perillat and Leo Lacroix as coaches. I learned, finally, how to carve a giant slalom turn in long sweeping runs down the glaciers above Val d'Isere and Tignes and enjoyed afternoon soccer matches with heroes of the 1968 Grenoble Olympics.

We traveled by air charter to Milan and train to the Alps and I vividly recall seeing uniformed Italians who were identified as members of the Italian communist party. I may have misunderstood this detail, but I do remember standing face-to-face with supposed communists and appreciating their humanity for the first time. They were slight, unimpressive individuals who seemed to share little with the great communist threat in the world.

During my trip, the second Vietnam draft lottery was held back home and I participated in absentia. My roommate at the ski camp was also of draft age and he called home—his father was a doctor in Pittsburgh, and Matt had the luxury of a car and international calling privileges—the morning after the draft to get the numbers corresponding with our birthdays. We talked in the days before about staying Europe if our numbers were below 50, as that most certainly meant we would be drafted, but he had a number well over 200 and mine was 186. When camp ended, he went on a road trip through Italy and I flew home, safe from the specter of the draft. I landed at Albany County Airport with a dime left in my pocket to call my dad for a ride home, probable evidence I never would have made it as an ex-pat in Europe.

My next visit 'across the pond' wouldn't be until 35 years later. Graduation from college, entering the job market, marriage and raising a family all conspired to delay the inevitable. That it took so long was not a lack of interest, but more a question of how "way leads on to way," in the words from Robert Frost's "The Road Not Taken." In the interim, I learned that Latvia was a land with a long history based, not on its sovereignty, but on the culture of the tribes which combine to make up modern-day Latvians. My German ancestors lived there in the middle of the 19th century during a long period of rule by the Russian Empire, but it was a time of growing national identity on the part of the ethnic Latvians. In the aftermath of World War I, with the support of Estonians, as well as Britain, France and much later, the U.S., the Republic of Latvia was formed, freeing them from the control of the Russian monarchists, German landowners and merchants, and assorted Bolsheviks. Unfortunately, independence was short-lived as Hitler and Stalin negotiated what became known as the Molotov-Ribbentrop Non-Aggression Pact in 1939, which spelled the end of Latvia as a free country. The irony drips from the pact's title, as it also opened the door for the beginning of World War II.

In addition to the history of the early 20th century, other obstacles kept us at arms-length from Latvia. Communication with any remaining family ended with Uncle Oscar's visit to Riga just after World War II, when he was told that his mother's aunts did not survive the war, ostensibly starved by the Nazis. He was given a few small embroidered items the current residents had saved after the aunts' passing, "we saved them in case someone asked about them." Of course, the Cold War of my youth extended into the late 1980s, and other than Uncle Oscar's intrepid visit, little opportunity to travel in Eastern Europe was available and other communication would be limited anyway. With Uncle Oscar's death in 1968 and Aunt Freida's in 1976, the last of their generation was gone. Dad's younger brother Paul, the reclusive lawyer who lived in Staten Island, NY, had far greater interest in our ancestry than Dad, insisting that ethnic Latvians inhabited the family tree (a claim Dad dismissed), but Paul died in 1975. His family records were apparently destroyed in a fire shortly before his death; his executor claiming none survived.

We had two brief hand-written pieces documenting the fathers of Oscar W. Maddaus and Augusta Dorothea Rathminder Maddaus. The former is a 4-line German listing for Johann Karl Ludwig Maddaus, attributed to the "Lexikon Baltischer Kunstler" (Directory of Baltic Artists), edited by Dr. Wilhelm Neumann and published in Riga in 1908. The English translation to the text indicates he was born in Hamburg in 1820, came to Riga in the early 1840s and worked as a portrait artist and lithographer until his death in Riga in 1878. The family oral history has it that Johann immigrated to Riga, at that time located in the Russian Empire, to avoid conscription in the Prussian Army.

A second listing for Andžs Rātminders, 1805-1887 is written in what is believed to Latvian—a note in the margin says 'not German.' A rough translation suggests that Andžs was headmaster/teacher in the community school in Vecpiebalga from 1823-1887, a total of 63 years. The listing is attributed to the "Latviju Enciplopedija" (Latvian Encyclopedia) by Arveds Svabe, published in Stockholm, Sweden, 1950. No further written information was passed down in the family regarding either of these patriarchs.

My father's reticence to discuss our ethnicity belied quite a treasure trove of knowledge nonetheless, and fortunately for our family, my older brother John took it upon himself to mine each and every nugget of information in preparation for a Maddaus Family reunion he organized for the summer of 1995. With additional input from my mother and second cousins Bill and John S., John composed a Family History of 21 pages, tracing in bullet point format the highlights of the known members of the family tree. The reunion that followed brought together many of the descendants of Oscar (Sr.) and Ingo (Sr.) Maddaus, the only two of the 6 siblings who came from Riga in 1883 and subsequently married and had children. Characteristically, the only surviving Maddaus who was a first generation American, my father, chose not to attend, avoiding one of his worst fears, and rightly so, of being the center of attention.

One of the most important pieces of information John discovered came, not from our parents, but from a co-worker of his at the University of Maine. John's colleague visited Latvia after the fall of the Soviet Union as part of a re-opening of the former Soviet republics to the west. We knew that our great great-grandfather, Johann Karl Ludwig Maddaus, was an artist in Riga and John prevailed on his colleague to use his contacts to search for any historical evidence of our ancestor. The response arrived a few weeks later from the director of the Latvian National Museum of Art, Māra Lace:

Riga,

June 16, 1995

Dear Mr. John Maddaus,

Mr. Juris Ubāns forwarded your letter to our Museum which we read with great interest.

The name of the painter Johann Karl Ludwig Maddaus is not unknown to us. There are two paintings by him in the collection of the State Museum of Fine Art:

> 1. Portrait of the Artist's Daughter Otilia Maddaus, Cardboard, oil, 61 x 50,5 (oval) No. GL – 1087
> 2. Self-portrait (?), Cardboard, oil, 30 x 24,5 (oval)! No. GL – 1123
>
> With best regards,
> Mara Lace
> Director of the State Museum of Fine Art

While the news was not a total surprise, I think this gave us the first insight to the fact that the two World Wars and the Soviet Occupation that followed did not totally obliterate all trace of our ancestry. The Republic of Latvia in 1995 had been independent only a few years as a result of the dissolution of the USSR and we now had tangible evidence of what the new country might hold. Still, I must admit that this could not totally overcome the perception that what had been behind the Iron Curtain was the darkness and evil of the Soviet period.

We received photos of the two portraits almost two years later and we got the first (and to this date, only) look at an image of our great, great-grandfather, the artist. We had no knowledge of Otilia (sic) (presumably Oscar W.'s sister) before receiving the letter from the art museum and it underscored how little we knew of Oscar W. and Augusta's families. Not only had a political Iron Curtain been drawn between America and the USSR, but a veil had been drawn between the Maddaus family in America and its roots in Latvia.

John subsequently became acquainted with University of Southern Maine Art Professor Juris Ubāns, who was born in Latvia, and wrote to Ubāns asking if he ever returned to Latvia and passed along this contact to me. Juris Ubāns, in addition to teaching art and art history is an accomplished artist, and also the son of one of the great early 20th century Latvian artists, Konrāds Ubāns, who was one of a small group who were instrumental in establishing the Latvian National Museum of Art (formerly known as the State Museum of Fine Art), just after the turn of the century. Through a number of emails, Ubāns was very helpful in my planning of my first venture to Latvia.

Chapter Four
A Flat World

My first opportunity to visit Latvia wouldn't come until 2005 and it really came as an afterthought. I had never worked in a job that afforded me enough income to travel a great deal, and my job as a high school English teacher was no different. After college, I had worked in a New Hampshire ski resort town for a few years, taking multiple jobs to stay alive, and married before I had what I'd call a real occupation. A house, children, and a management training position in banking followed, and then before I knew it, divorce, severance from banking due to the consolidations of the early 1990s, and finally, single-parenthood, led me to high school teaching as an occupation in desperation. In spite of the way I entered education, and the immediate need to be re-trained to earn certification, it became a good fit for me and after 10 years, I was continually looking to expand my skills.

One of the drawbacks of teaching is the fact that high school teachers are steered towards professional development in pedagogy, curriculum, and technology, leaving little opportunity to pursue additional studies in their discipline. I finally decided that the latter needed attention, and then got lucky. The alumni office at Bates College, my alma mater, advertised a scholarship program for teachers. Called the Barlow Alumni Travel Grant, it seemed to be an excellent opportunity to expand my horizons, and so I applied and before long was notified that, indeed, I would receive the grant. My proposal was to study Shakespeare for two weeks in a summer program at Cambridge University in England and apply the knowledge to my classroom teaching. In planning my summer study, it occurred to me: why not take an extra week and visit

Latvia? A quick check of my finances and research of the additional costs, led me to the conclusion that finally I would be visiting the land of my ancestors.

The spring of 2005 marked the publication of Thomas L. Friedman's "The World Is Flat," aptly subtitled "A Brief History of the Twenty-First Century," and I read through his work with great interest. Increasingly, I began to look at my visit to Latvia through the lens of his 'Flat World.' Friedman cites three important dates in his 'history' and one of the three is obvious to even the most casual of readers—9/11/2001—the date of the attacks on the World Trade Center and the Pentagon. While this date didn't have a direct impact on making Latvia more accessible to me (I was nervous in that I left for London two days after the subway bombings in July 2005, but managed to skirt the area most effected), the other two dates, which are the first two of what he terms 'The 10 Forces Which Flattened the World, ' had a dramatic impact.

The first of Friedman's Flatteners is 11/09/1989, a curious inversion of the 9/11 date we have come to know so well. November 9, 1989 was the date of the fall of the Berlin Wall, precipitating the fall of the Soviet Union and the opening of Eastern Europe to communication with the Western World. I had experienced this already through receiving the information from the Latvian National Museum of Art, and the flow of general information relating to Latvia which followed. Restoration of Latvian independence didn't take place until mid-1991, and came as the result of a coup d'état in Moscow, and it took a number of years before Russian troops left the country, but finally Latvia, which had been independent between 1920 and 1940, was once again free of the Russian bear. Independence has not been without complications, as a large minority of ethnic Russians live primarily in the cities and ethnic tension manifests itself in politics and business, but Latvia was admitted to the European Union and NATO in 2004 and has a westward bent.

The second of Friedman's Flatteners—8/09/1995—has had a subtle but dramatic effect on my research. This was the date that Netscape (remember that name from ancient digital history?) went public, and as

Friedman notes "the first mainstream browser—and the whole culture of Web browsing for the general public—was created by a tiny company in Mountain View, California." The impact for me was multifaceted. Over the ten years that followed, I could surf the Web for information about Latvia and—unbelievably, to me—my ancestors, I could contact total strangers to follow up on the information, and I could be contacted by total strangers who were curious about my surname. The latter was perhaps the most interesting, although all three have been extremely valuable.

One example of being contacted via the Internet occurred in 2004, when a woman named Eileen Marcil from Quebec City in Canada contacted my mother and me, looking for information about her Maddaus ancestor. My father, who was still alive though bed-ridden as a result of a stroke, was immediately suspicious of this contact, thinking all she wanted was money. We ultimately learned that her German Granny, Adolphine Dorothea Caroline Winterhof, was the daughter of Johanne Christina Maddaus, younger sister of Johann Karl Ludwig, making Eileen and my father 4th cousins. Eileen sent us quite a bit of the research she had done on the Maddaus family in Hamburg giving us further insight into Johann's upbringing and decision to move to Riga as a young man. Eileen has cousins in both England and New Zealand and passed along the story the Bremners of New Zealand had heard from their grandmother that Johann had painted for the Czar of Russia and the Spanish court. While I have not been able to confirm this, I keep it in mind as my research deepens.

A second example of the power of the Internet was a contact from an author named James Haas of Annapolis Maryland whose extensive research on the German industrialist Conrad Poppenhusen had uncovered the work of an artist named 'O. Maddaus.' Poppenhusen had a share of the patents for rubber manufacturing with the Goodyear brothers and built a fortune on the India Rubber Comb Company in College Point NY, before he and his sons lost it investing in the Long Island Railroad. 'O. Maddaus' was determined to be Oscar W. Maddaus, my great-grandfather (and the son of Johann Maddaus) who apparently learned his trade as a woodcut artist from his father and established his roots in America working not only for Poppenhusen's company, but also Remington Sewing Machine and Reed and Barton Flatware Company. Haas noted that Poppenhusen was from Hamburg and that Hamburgers tended to stick together, suggesting that Johann and his son moved with liked-minded Hamburg merchants to Riga and New York City, respectively, in a sort of 19th century net-working. Oscar W. died in 1896 and little was known of him in our family, until Haas and the Internet made the information easily available.

By the time my Shakespeare course was over in Cambridge and I hopped on my Ryanair flight from London-Stansted to Riga Lidosta (airport), I had developed a fair amount of information about Johann Karl Ludwig Maddaus, but I would find that the Internet is no substitute for being there. I have returned a dozen additional times in the past decade and each time a new layer of our ancestry is unfolded. Each piece of information has led to new questions, both with regard to the Maddaus ancestry and the Rathminder ancestry, and although the former has been interesting, the latter has led me into the fabric of Latvian culture and to the realization that despite the 120+ years that have passed since Oscar W. and Augusta left Riga for the American experience, two horrific World Wars and 50 years of brutal Soviet occupation, Rathminder relatives have survived and are now flourishing in Latvia.

Chapter Five

Latvia - July 2005

As much as I anticipated my first visit to Latvia, it wasn't without some trepidation. The past history of the Soviet occupation of the country from 1944 through 1991 or so had me wondering what remnants of the communist world would remain, how an American would be treated and how I would communicate in a Latvian and Russian-speaking country, knowing only English. I was still conditioned by crawling under flimsy desks during grade-school air raid drills, draft status concerns in high school and college years during the Vietnam War, and the constant drone of Communist Domino Theory in American politics had not been wiped clean by the fall of the Berlin Wall, even though that event was now over a decade removed.

I stayed the first few days in a Russian guest-house not far from the Latvian National Museum of Art, the main target of my visit, and was given some idea of the city by a Russian English teacher/friend of the owners. I had the vague sense that she was looking for a husband to take her out of Latvia, as she had been born in Russia and only had resident-alien status in Latvia. She must have decided I wasn't a good candidate because after a short tour of the old city she left me to my own resources and did not meet me the next day as promised. I contemplated the concept of being rejected by a Russian gold-digger for a moment and continued on with my itinerary, without further thought

The present unrest in the World, especially the Middle East, largely due to the conflict between America and forces of Islamic terrorism, was palpable. Two weeks removed from the London subway bombings, and with wars in Afghanistan and Iraq, America was not regarded as a universally benevolent actor on the world stage and American security efforts had exacerbated its role.

One of the early examples of this was the security around the US Embassy in Riga, located in the city center on Raina iela (iela is Latvian for street). I was encouraged by the State Department website to check in at the Embassy upon arrival and I found numerous layers of security around the building. I stopped to take a picture of the building, an act of national pride, I guess, and was immediately confronted with an armed guard who advised me in emphatic terms to not, under any circumstances, take any photos of the Embassy. Later, on my trip in Berlin and Munich, similar beefed-up security was evident at American diplomatic locations. The US Embassy in Latvia was moved a few years later to a more secure site on the edge of the city not too far from the airport.

I did get a nice tour of the Old City, the canal separating it from the commercial city center, a view from high above the city from the observation tower at St. Peter's Church and a short walk along the Daugava River. At no point did I feel the slightest bit uncomfortable, and I immediately noticed some English spoken among the clash of Latvian and Russian conversation, which I could not distinguish between. On the drive into the city, I had sensed the change in architecture from what I refer to as Soviet block-housing to the older European decorative style I would later learn to be Art Nouveau.

I had arranged an appointment the second day at the Latvian National Museum of Art with the Head of Collections and Scientific Research (18th – 1st half of the 20th century) Department—an impressive title, indeed. After introductions, Aija took me to an unused exhibition room and where she had arranged not two, but three works of Johann Karl Ludwig Maddaus from their collection. These included the self-portrait and a portrait of a young woman—his daughter Ottilie—both in oil, and a lithograph portrait of a church leader. The lithograph was a surprise, as we had not known of a third work in their collection. Aija explained that the artist was indeed listed in the Baltic German

Artist directory and that apparently the works had been donated posthumously by his wife.

Johann Maddaus artwork in LNMA, 2005

Without a background in art or art history and noticing the somewhat aged look and relative modest size of the works and their frames, I felt a sense of awe, mixed with a bit of consternation. Here were three works of my great, great grandfather held in the collection of a national art museum, but not in the permanent exhibition and not especially impressive in their presentation. And yet, here also was my ancestor, in effect speaking to me over the decades since his son left Riga in 1883. I couldn't intuit the sound of the voice but I heard, 'here I am, and you have returned to see me and my work.' The one hundred, twenty-two years that had intervened, and the three thousand, eight hundred miles that I'd traveled, dissolved into a present face-to-face with my great, great grandfather, a man I knew so little about. And yet through his self-portrait, his entire being touched me.

Sensing the uniqueness in my experience, Aija urged me to stay as long I liked to view the works and left me alone in the room for a while. (I've since met with her at least a half dozen times, run into her in the museum hallways, even seen her at a local restaurant—and every time she as gracious as can be, a wonderful caretaker for our ancestor's works.) I took a number of photos of the works from every possible angle, it seemed, and after her return and a short parting conversation, I left the museum.

I'm not sure being brought up fully American in the US, that I, or anyone for that matter, would have any concept of what it would be like to travel to Europe, much less behind the former Iron Curtain, and to see artwork created by an ancestor. It's not something many of us would ever consider, much less experience. And so, I had done it, and it felt a little like shedding a layer of skin or uncovering a treasure under a stone. Nothing had really changed, and yet I felt changed.

I returned to the Russian guest house for a second night. The next day I would be in a Latvian Homestay on the city outskirts, preparing for day trips to the countryside, one to Vecpiebalga in Latvia, the second across the border to Paistu, Estonia.

Chapter Six

The Road to Vecpiebalga

My first road trip from Riga into the Latvian countryside took some preparation, as you can imagine. I had already queried Juris Ubāns about driving in Latvia, and he assured me—with a bit of humor—that I would not find it all that different from Maine. (And as it turns out, Latvia is generally not all that different from Maine.) I planned ahead with a contact and reservation with the Hertz Latvia office where Arturs, the manager assured me that there would be no problem. (I have rented from the same agency, usually dealing with Arturs directly at least 10 times and hesitate to look for a cheaper alternative, the service is so good.) On arrival at the Hertz office in the Old City, Arturs did advise me of a delay in arrival of my car. It seems that business was so good, they had to buy a new Toyota Corolla Hatchback—a model I would love to see in the U.S.—to fill my order. A sign of the times, no doubt, as the growth of business from joining the European Union and NATO had positive effects on the local economy.

Making my way out of the city on Brivibas iela (Freedom Boulevard), I eventually found myself headed east on the A2 highway, towards the Piebalga region 100km east of the capital. The destination is a village called Vecpiebalga. (VETS'-pee-a-balg) 'Piebalga' means 'by the river' the small river running through the region and 'vec' is old. Jaunpiebalga, the new village, is 10km further northeast. The trip required a 100km drive straight east-northeast on highway A2 and 35km south on a local paved road, P30.

My great grandmother, Augusta Dorothea Rathminder Maddaus, left little evidence of her family beyond one academic reference from

Arveds Svabes' encyclopedia of Latvia. Her father—or so we thought—was Andžs Rātminders (Latvian spelling—Rathminder is the German version), who was noted in the national register as serving as a schoolteacher in Vecpiebalga for 63 years (1823-1886), admired for his longevity and the incredible variety of notable students he had during the period. I hoped to be lucky enough to find a trace, but was in no way prepared for what I found. Certainly, I had no idea that, years later, I would be attending a pagan celebration of Midsummer's night with distant cousins, attending a national song and dance festival with thousands of Latvians or pouring through Latvian literature for information written by or about my ancestors. But that came a few years later.

The first landmark on the right entering Vecpiebalga from the north is the Skolas kapi, literally, the 'school cemetery,' so-named for its closeness to the local k12 school. I had no specific landmarks in mind and the cemetery in the center of the village seemed a likely place to start, so I set out walking through the graveyard reading gravestones. This is not something I'd recommend as the most effective way to research ancestry but it was all I had. After 10 or 15 minutes, I came upon a familiar name on one good sized monument: Kaudzitis. It was the memorial stone for the authors Reinis and Matīss Kaudzītis, credited with over 30 books in a variety of genres, including "Time of the Land Surveyors" (in Latvian, "Mērnieku Laiki"), one of the first Latvian language novels. The second name on the monument was that of Matīss's wife, "Līze Kaudzitis, nee Rathminderis." Could Līze be from the same family as my great grandmother?

The monument was located in a typical plot of roughly measuring 15x30, containing 5 markers and surrounded by cedar and other undergrowth. Turning away from the Kaudzitis monument, I scanned the facing stone which read:

> Vecpieblagas
> draudjes skolotajs
> Unzchs Rathminders
> 6 mart 1805 t 30 dec 1886
> Umata bijis 63 gadas
> ==================
> Ede Rathminders, dz Kornets
> 28 jan 1813 t 6 dec 1899

This was the grave of 'Vecpiebalga's friendly schoolteacher, Andžs Rātminders and his wife Ede Kornet Ratmindere.

At the grave of Andžs and Ede Rathminder, Skolas kapi, Vecpiebalga, 2005

My great, great grandfather and grandmother!? I cannot explain in words the feeling I had coming face-to-face with this monument, but I remember feeling a sense of fortune in finding this so easily and satisfaction that the trip was worth making. I had no indication of this graveyard or gravestone in any of my research, and yet here it was, and I, standing before it!

At the top, the memorial came to a cross with the inscription, in Latvian, from 1 John 3:14--"We know that we have left death and come over into life; we know it because we love others."

I drew a sketch of this section of the graveyard, noting the names on the 4 or 5 other monuments in the plot, as best I could, given the varying age and wear on each one. After composing myself and taking a couple of dozen pictures, I returned to the car for my next stop, Kalna Kaibeni ('On top of the hill'), the home of the Kaudzites, 6 or so kilometers from the center of the village.

I spent two or so hours touring the museum, the oldest of its kind in Latvia, dating to just after Matīss' death in 1926, and talking to the caretaker, an amiable man named Dzintars, "Amber" for short. He spoke little English but had the most interesting reaction when we compared the photo I had of my great grandmother Augusta with the museum's picture of Līze Ratmindere-Kaudzīte--"sister." The resemblance was indeed remarkable.

Amber had no photocopier but let me copy by hand information about Līze Kaudzite and her father and gave me one long biography of him, in Latvian of course, in which his five daughters were listed: Marija, Anna, Maija, Līze and Karline. In comparing the names to those of the other 3 grave markers from the cemetery, I determined that these were all markers of the son-in-law's family names, Tullijs (Antons--a teacher and poet), Jurjanu (Dr. J) and Scharsberg (a merchant).

In all the biographical information, one name was missing---Augusta Dorothea Rathminder. With this missing link so stark, I remembered that I had found another Rātminders by the name of Jānis. Amber helped me find his name in Andžs' biography, listed as an author, teacher and younger brother of Andžs.

I left Vecpiebalga with the sense of accomplishment, but with a huge unanswered question—who was Augusta's father and why is she not mentioned in Andžs' biographical information. Was it due to her departure to America with my great grandfather? Or was she the niece of Andžs Rātminders?

It would take more research and a number of trips to Latvia to find the answer. Either way, I left Vecpiebalga this first time with the feeling that I had walked the same ground as my ancestors and their spirits were undeniably present.

Chapter Seven

Paistu, Estonia

After my day trip to Vecpiebalga and second night at Homestay, I'd gotten to know the owner well enough to get a sense of my way around the outskirts of Riga and the Mezaparks (Forest Park) area the B&B was located in. The inn had no sign and sat on a fenced-in area in an upscale neighborhood. Diga, the owner was ethnic Latvian, and her husband, Rick, a New Zealander, and they had a handful of pets who shared the space. It was a delightful way to spend my evenings and while they didn't serve dinner, she directed me to a wonderful restaurant a few blocks away called Gustavs Adolfs, which has been a favorite through the years.

The trip to Estonia involved headed back out the A2, north on A1 and, once crossing the border, a winding route on Estonian highways to the city of Viljandi, with Paistu located just 5 or 6 kilometers outside the city. This would be my one and only controlled border crossing, as the establishment of the Schengen Zone would eliminate border controls a few years later.

I arranged to attend the 2:00 PM Sunday worship service through a series of emails with the Mary's church secretary and was met by she and the pastor immediately on my arrival. Neither spoke English, nor did I speak Estonian, but soon a local schoolteacher, who was fluent in English, arrived to translate for us. Pastor Raivo noted that he had been to Washington, DC and Florida during a short trip to America a few years earlier and was now retired from his role as a military chaplain.

Mary's Church dates to the late 13th century, and sits on the high point of a long, gradually upward sloping farmland community of

Paistu, surrounded by willows and a small village square. The church office was in a house along one of the side streets. Pastor Raivo explained the congregation was small—only a dozen or so attended the service—but the church had some support for renovation of the roof in recent years and the altar painting, most recently. The church organ would have to wait for its refurbishment.

The painting, "Kristus ristil," in Estonian, "Christ on the Cross" in English, was well documented on various internet sites and was the first I had found at the outset of my search for additional works of Johann Karl Ludwig Maddaus. I had seen pictures online, but was not prepared for the real thing.

Mary's Church altar, Paistu, Estonia

Centered inside the altar area, which itself is surrounded by a 3-foot-high communion rail, the painting stands 6-7 feet high and 4 feet wide above the communion table. The restoration was evident in the sheen and brightness of the colors. I will include photos and description in a later section of this work, but will say at this point, the work is as impressive as any altar painting I have ever seen.

I enjoyed following the Estonian language order of worship, much like the Lutheran liturgy in English, and even though I had no idea of what specifically was being said. There's a musicality and rhythm that is unmistakable.

We enjoyed coffee and deserts in the parish office after the service and I experienced a feeling that would be repeated a number of times over the convening years. I was the honored guest, the prodigal son, a representative in the present of a revered time in history when the church had received a blessing in the form of the artist's work. Although I could take no credit for my part in it, I did feel bathed in the admiration and regard for my ancestor.

I have heard the story of how the painting made its way to Paistu from Riga in more than one iteration, and each is slightly different from the other, but this is as close as I can get to it:

The pastor of the church in the late 1840s had a merchant friend in Riga who he was very close to and at one point the daughter of the merchant asked her father if they could make a gift to the pastor in his new church in Paistu. The daughter talked to her siblings and friends and created a fund for this purpose, which the merchant supplemented with earnest money to make the gift a reality. The painting was contracted with Johann Maddaus, completed in 1852 and before it left Riga, it was put on display at St. John's Church in what is now the Old City.

To transport the painting, a farmer from Holstre, a town near Paistu, offered to travel the 160 kilometers or so with his horses and wagon to bring the painting to Mary's Church. This would be quite a distance for horse and wagon at any point in history and 1852 would be no exception. And so, due to the feelings of a young girl, the volunteerism of a local farmer and over the obstacle of great distance, the painting arrived in Paistu and has graced the altar ever since.

Unfortunately, tragedy struck in both Riga and Holstre. The merchant's daughter, who was so instrumental in the gift of the painting, became ill and died before it could be completed. And two weeks after the long trip to Riga brought the painting to Paistu, the farmer's barn burned down, taking the lives of both horses.

"Kristus ristil," in spite of its tragic origins and the troubled history of the Baltics, endures among the small congregation in rural Estonia. While we have no ancestral connection with Estonia, I still think of Paistu often, as a caretaker for my great, great-grandfather's legacy.

Chapter Eight

Return from Latvia

After my drives to the countryside, I spent another day in Riga and night at the Homestay. I rode the #11 tram into the City Center for the afternoon, walked for miles through the parks along the canal, had crepes at a Latvian restaurant called Provence in the Old City and generally enjoyed myself without further research into ancestry. I just took in the experience. Riga is delightful for that purpose, if nothing else.

The trip home involved a couple stops in Germany to visit friends in Berlin and Stuttgart, before taking a shuttle to London for the final flight home.

Visiting Berlin was fascinating in part due to recent history, the Wall, Checkpoint Charlie, the Brandenburg Gate, the Bundestag, and a number of other sites, and in large part due to my tour guide and friend Stefan, a lifelong resident. Stefan was completing an internship in the foreign affairs ministry of Parliament as part of his legal studies, and he's an astute student of politics, history and architecture. I could not have had a better two days in Germany's capital.

The next stop featured another tour guide and friend, Jochen, who along with his wife Julia, gave me a glimpse of Stuttgart, plus a couple adventures beyond the city. While Jochen spent a day studying—also legal studies—Julia drove me to visit the school in Rottburg, where she was an elementary teacher, and then to the village of Schweberdingen, where my mother's maternal grandmother's Behringer ancestors lived in the mid-19th century. There, in a visit to the local church, I saw my maternal great, great grandfather's baptismal noted in the church records.

Jochen and I took a road trip the next day, first by autobahn to Munich at 220kph in his father's Mercedes M-class SUV, then to Mittelburg, Austria, where we would climb the Widderstein the next day. Highlights included eating weisswurst at a street side café and hearing the Glochenspiel in the center of Munich, visiting the 1972 Olympic venues and the Spitz pool and climbing the observation tower for a view of the city spreading out in all directions.

Crossing the border from Oberstdorf to a small section of Austria accessible by car only from Germany, we enjoyed the Hotel Alte Krone tucked in to the Kleinvalsertal Valley and prepared for our climb of the 9000-foot Widderstein. My first experience in the European Alps gave me the perspective of the high meadows where local farmers live and pasture their sheep, the interconnected valleys crisscrossed with ski lifts, and the huts scattered at elevation to service a variety of hiker, climbers and trampers. The final climb was a tough as I could imagine—steep and treacherous—without use of ropes. And the summit was a dramatic and awe-inspiring as any I have reached. A truly outstanding climb!

A short flight later and I was back in London and a 12-hour layover. No point in not taking advantage of the stop! I checked my luggage with British Airways and took the train to the city, walked along the Thames and even took in an afternoon performance of Shakespeare's "Timon of Athens" at the Globe Theatre, a marvelously modern and visually engaging show viewed as I leaned on the stage in the wastrel section. Not wanting to leave, I pulled myself away in time to return to the 'tube' and the ride back to Heathrow for the flight home.

Caught in rush-hour traffic with half of London's workers on their way home would be hectic enough had the entire London subway system been in working order, but this was only three weeks or so after the London Subway Bombings and half the loop was out of service. This was just another reminder that communism had been replaced by radical Islamic terrorism as the primary enemy of the 'free-world'. The ride back to meet the train to Heathrow was doubly crowded, such that moving was nearly impossible. Combined with a change in trains I wasn't entirely sure of, my return was somewhat harrowing, and Heathrow a welcome site as I arrived with an hour to spare.

During my flight home, I had time to reflect on all that I'd seen: Cambridge, Berlin, Stuttgart, Munich, the Widderstein and London, all marvelous stops on a fantastic trip, but all that time I knew that Riga and Latvia would be the most likely destinations I would revisit and at this writing it is the only one.

Chapter Nine

Back to Latvia - August 2009

Another four years have passed and I am back in Latvia for a second visit. Considering my elevated interest in my heritage the interval has been long, but yet much has transpired since my first journey to the Baltics and not all related to family research.

Once again, 'way would lead on to way,' but this interval would be much shorter.

Taking your son to college for his freshman year took on new meaning for me later in 2005, as Jacob decided he'd had enough of Maine and wanted to venture beyond the state's borders to start his college career. So, he chose New Zealand. It is a long story, but to be brief, he remembered my summer camp counselor friend David, and asked if I would contact him for information about New Zealand universities. By late October, we were on a plane to Wellington for Jacob's first term at Victoria University. It was the summer term and he would stay for the fall term as well, before transferring to Northeastern University in Boston for the balance of his undergraduate studies.

The trip to New Zealand led to my interest in schools there, and before I flew home, I had acquired a teaching position. The following year was marked by teaching English at Gore High School in the Southland of the South Island, a truly transformational professional experience. As the saying goes, "absence makes the heart grow fonder," and after 5+ months it was apparent that returning home was necessary. And happily, Beth and I were married less than two months later.

New Zealand's focus on literacy prompted me to enroll in a Master's program at the University of Maine, to delve more deeply into the concept. And with a new life in both marriage and education, Latvia faded somewhat in my consciousness. Or would have, if not for the internet.

The next three years included finishing climbing the 4000-footers in New Hampshire, Maine and Vermont, 67 in all, attending Beth's brother's wedding in Chile, keeping up with all six of the children in our blended family and taking a succession of graduate courses at the University of Maine (thanks to the hospitality of my brother John), while continuing to teach High School English. But with the World Wide Web ever at my fingertips, I learned enough new and interesting information about Johann Karl Ludwig Maddaus and Latvia, that, by 2009, a second trip to Latvia became an imperative I could not ignore. Fortunately, Beth signed on for the adventure and became an invaluable asset and partner in my continued search.

The second visit was facilitated by a fair amount of internet research and made much more pleasant with the company of Beth, who has to be the most amiable and accepting travel partner in the world. I give her a lot of credit for encouraging my research and travels and then joining me for so many of my adventures. I would like to say all I need to do is mention birds that we might see on route, but she seems to enjoy our travel partnership regardless.

Knowing at least some of Johann Maddaus' history and having more clues to the Rathminder ancestry gave me plenty of options when deciding what to enter in the search field on Google, and added Latvian and Estonian spellings of the family names along with the discovery of google.lv and google.es search engines, which opened up a plethora of new leads. By the time we headed for Stockholm in August of 2009, I had quite an itinerary set for our new Baltic adventure.

While I enjoy the experience of being a tourist, I am much more motivated to make specific connections in my travels. Going to major or minor league baseball games in different cities, attending concerts—I've seen the Canadian band Blue Rodeo in three Canadian provinces and England—and seeking out unique aspects of a city or National park all appeal to me more than the usual tourist sites, and with a few exceptions, I prefer self-guided discovery to guided tours.

I had most of our Latvia itinerary planned except for the connecting flight from Stockholm to Riga, when Beth as she often does, interjected a unique alternative. We were faced with a night in Stockholm and a flight the next morning across the Baltic Sea, but her solution combined the two. After a little research and we had booked overnight passage on the Tallink Silja Line's Romantika, a daily cruise vessel/ferry, popular with many Latvians and Russians, and just the perfect ticket after our long flight from Boston.

Romantika follows a circuitous route from the Port of Stockholm at Vartan Harbor through the beautiful channels and islands to the Baltic Sea. Our late afternoon departure with a bright sun and under puffy clouds afforded us such sensational vistas we nearly missed our dinner. Later, in our cabin we sensed the easy undulation of the open sea, as it rocked us to sleep.

The morning arrival in Latvia is well-timed with the onboard breakfast. Just as we finished, the coast came in to view and the ship entered the mouth of the Daugava River. We had just enough time to retrieve our bags from our cabin and return to the deck to see the Riga city skyline appear on the east bank of the river.

Our boutique hotel in the Old City was a short cab ride from the terminal, although the Russian cabbie I chose took an extended route to our destination to pad the fare, a lesson I learned too late, but has been instructive in subsequent visits. We had much of the day open to rest up and tour the Old City before the serious family history tour would begin.

In the four years since my first visit, I had found additional Johann Maddaus paintings through a google search and one site especially which reviewed a new four-volume encyclopedic series, "The Lutheran Churches of Latvia" ("Latvijas luternu baznicas"), by Vitolds Mašnovskis. The reference to a Maddaus altar painting in Carnikava, outside Riga, led me to purchase of three of the four volumes.

Mašnovskis' work is detailed, comprehensive and attractively laid out with photography and artwork to document each of the 300 or so Lutheran Churches in the country. With Johann Maddaus mentioned in the text of Carnikava, Garkalne, Turaida, and Tirza churches, I set out to contact pastors of each and was successful in three out of the four.

I also planned a return to the Latvian National Museum of Art to see the three works I first saw in 2005, with the understanding that the portrait of the artist's daughter, Ottilie, had undergone restoration. A final stop would be a return to the Paistu church in Estonia, giving us a complete update on my research and Beth a first glimpse of the Maddaus Ancestry Tour. As with each visit, before and after, new questions and insights would present themselves, sometimes at the most unexpected times.

Aija, at the National Museum of Art, greeted us graciously, as always, and produced the self-portrait once again for my inspection and photographing. She explained that Ottilie was not available, as the painting had been loaned to an exhibition of 19th Century portraiture being held at the Rundale Palace, some 80 kilometers south of Riga, near the Lithuanian border. Fortunately, we had an extra day open with our rental car, and so Rundale was added to our plans. Aija also indicated that the Self-Portrait would be added to the list of works needing restoration and I made a mental note to follow-up with her on that.

Our first road trip, though would be to meet with the pastor of the church in Carnikava. He offered to take us to Garkalne as well, which was close by, and to his other church in Baltezers. Pastor Gundars was about forty, married with a young son, well-versed in the history of both the churches involved and, fortunately for us, fluent in English.

We drove past the Baltezers church where Pastor Gundars had his office, and visited Garkalne first, where I had set up a meeting with the church rector. Here, in a secluded wooded setting, the small white church set on a slight bluff, above the gravel road leading into the village.

The rector explained that the lower altar painting was the one we wanted to see, but had little information about how the congregation had acquired it. It is a reproduction of da Vinci's "The Last Supper," and gave me some new insight into Johann Maddaus' craft as an artist. Well-established as a portrait painter, he was often asked to reproduce great works of other established artists and da Vinci and Rubens were two he was often asked to 'copy.' How he managed to do so during the mid-19th century from a relatively remote city on the Baltic Sea, became a question I wouldn't answer until years later.

We continued to Carnikava and finally Baltezers, without seeing another Maddaus painting. Beth recorded the day as follows:

> This morning a Lutheran pastor who Charlie had corresponded with came and met us at our hotel to take us to see the site of a church that had one of Johann Maddaus' paintings on its altar. Foreshadowing: note the word "had" in the previous sentence.
>
> He pointed out a little church in the woods (near our hotel in Mezaparks, in the outskirts of Riga) as we drove past it and told us that in 1987, when he was a teenager, he read an article in Soviet Youth magazine about the pastor of this church who knew karate. He indicated that while the article was meant to ridicule the man and his congregation, he was intrigued and set out to visit the church. At that time in Latvia (what the Latvians refer to as Soviet Times) there were few churches and the ones that existed were full of KGB. Only four years later, freedom flowed through his country and they were all free to worship and to speak without fear. This pastor told us that he and many other of the current Latvian Lutheran pastors came out of that congregation.
>
> Today, this man pastors two churches. One that has been restored from its days serving as a factory for the Soviets and the other which has not yet been restored but where services are held twice a month. It is this un-restored church where we believe one of Charlie's great-grandfather's paintings was over the altar. Whether it is in storage with some of the other artifacts saved from churches before they were turned into factories, we were not entirely clear about. I hope so.

Churches into factories

Cemeteries into roads

The systematic destruction of a culture.

Here today, even with the hardships of the difficult economic climate you can feel the energy of a culture pulling things out of the attic and digging their memories out of storage.

In Carnikava, the church was an electronics factory, in Baltezers, the church was a chemicals storage facility. We found through this experience and later in Tirza, that the Communists used a variety of tactics to subvert the churches. In some cases, where congregations were somewhat strong, taxes would be levied to drain the church of its resources before it would be occupied for state use. Others were taken without pretense. Often the use would justify the seizure, with the alternative purpose the elimination of any faith gathering.

Carnikavas Lutheran church, 2009

Many of the churches had been restored beautifully, as in Baltezers, or are still undergoing the process, as in Carnikava, depending of the availability of government cultural funding or private resources. The congregations themselves had more difficulty in restoring their place in their communities. Many had dwindled to a handful of parishioners due to the long Soviet occupation and oppression.

A chance contact with a Latvian-American led to a referral to Raduraksti.lv, a digital record of various historical records from Latvian history, and I had spent some time perusing Riga Lutheran Church records, finding Johann Karl Ludwig Maddaus and family among two of the largest churches, St. Peter's and the Dome Church.

I had followed up with the Evangelical Lutheran Church of Latvia's church consistory where the Head of the Commission of Foreign Affairs was helpful in another reference to Eižens Upmanis of the German War Graves Commission who had, indeed, found our ancestors burial site in the Lielie kapi, or Great Cemetery. I arranged a meeting with Mr. Upmanis for our second day in Riga and he provided a wealth of information, although not what I expected.

Eižens took us first to the Great Cemetery, about 3 kilometers from the Old City, located there in 1773 in response to Catherine the Great's edict in the 18th Century that cemeteries in the Russian Empire be thus removed from city centers, as it was believed they were the source of bubonic plaque epidemics of 1770-1772. Many of the buried were Baltic Germans of the 18th and 19th centuries. Lielie kapi, as it's known in Latvian, is now fully part of the city and even borders a new, hip area known by its main street, Miera iela. The cemetery was desecrated by the Soviet Occupation force and officially designated a city park in 1967, although a few assorted headstones, in varying condition, still remain.

*Lielie kapi with Eižens Upmanis
at location of Johann Maddaus cemetery plot*

Using copies of cemetery plans, Eižens, paced from the front of the chapel to the spot, in a slightly overgrown section of the park, indicated the location of the Maddaus family plot. Included in the records were the names of Johann, his wife Adele, sons Alexander and August, and August's second wife, Wera. No stone marked the plot, nor were any others located nearby, the closest perhaps 50 feet away. Shaded by numerous deciduous trees, the undergrowth of hearty weeds choked out the possibility of grass. Eižens indicated that it was possible to have a stone erected on our ancestors' grave and offered to follow-up with me on this after our return to the U.S.

The chapel nearby, the Church of the Resurrection (Augšāmcelšanās Luterāņu baznīca) that looked out over the scene had also fallen into disrepair during the occupation, but had been restored after independence was regained in 1991 to honor many of those who had been deported to Siberia. A Cross made of rails from the railway to Siberian deportation adorns the outside of the chapel.

As we talked, it became apparent that Eižens was also a tremendous resource for all things Latvian, outside of graves and cemeteries. Trained as an architect and from a family of renowned architects, he had a great interest in the Art Nouveau style which permeates the city. As we left Lielie kapi, he offered to give us a tour of the prominent Art Nouveau areas of the city and take us to the newly established Art Nouveau Museum on Alberta Iela, managed by his wife. With little on our agenda for the rest of the day we agreed and from that point we received a tutorial on the architectural wonders of Riga, as well as a number of other subjects I have long forgotten. His enthusiasm and devotion to a variety of subjects was remarkable.

Before long we were sharing family histories and avocational interests. At one point, I mentioned upcoming visits to rural churches in Latvia and Estonia where Johann Maddaus altar paintings were located, including Tirza, a small village in central Vidzeme. Before I could explain further, he was on the phone to an architect friend who had a country home in Tirza and was active in the church. The conversation went somewhat like this:

> Eižens: "Nils, I am meeting with the great, great grandson of the artist who painted the Tirza church altar painting. He says he will be traveling there on Saturday"
>
> Nils: "Yes, we know and we are planning a celebration in honor of the artist."

Of course, I had arranged a visit with the pastor some weeks before, although I was not aware of the party we would soon take part in. This would be my first realization that in Latvia, most everything is connected in some way.

Eižens and I shared details of our immediate families, and he offered that he had two sons, giving some information about their careers and activities, and a daughter, Māra: 'she thinks she will be a rock star.' He said this with a combination of pride and doubt, as if I would not be as impressed, not knowing my interest in music. I would soon find that Māra Upmane and her band "Astro'n'out" was very popular in Latvia and even had a song of the year with "Daļa Rīgas" (A Part of Riga) a few years earlier. I have enjoyed her many recordings and even had a chance to see the band once in person.

I will note, as of this writing, Eižens Upmanis succumbed to cancer, much to my sadness. He had spent his last years negotiating between the church, which had neither the resources nor the willing membership, and the city, over the ownership and maintenance of the cemetery, without resolution. A new tram-line proposal by the city would encroach on the property and created further difficulty in negotiating an agreement. As one friend commented, his devotion to Lielie kapi may, in part, been his demise.

With the new knowledge of our ancestor's gravesite, Art Nouveau Architecture and Style and popular Latvian music, we took the next day to visit Rundale Palace and the portrait exhibition, with limited expectations. I wanted to see the Ottilie portrait restoration and knew Rundale was an interesting attraction, and we planned a stop at Bauska Castle, another attraction in the south-central Zemgale region.

Rundale Palace dates back to the 15th Century, but the current structure was designed and built in the mid-1700s on the plans of the Florentine architect Francesco Bartolomeo Rastrelli, who was based in St. Petersburg and known for designing the Winter Palace there, as well as quite a catalog of other majestic, Late Baroque structures, including one other in Latvia, Jelgava Palace. Most recently the Rundale has undergone a restoration which was in process when we visited and later completed in 2014. The expansive Palace and its gardens evoke Versailles in its scope and grandeur.

The Portrait Exhibition made ample use of the restored portion of the first floor of Palace made use of some 500 works, which have since been catalogued in a volume titled, "Portrets Latvija 19.gadsimts" ("Latvian Portraits of the 19th Century"). As with the Palace itself, we were unprepared for the sheer volume and beauty of the collection.

Making our way through the many adjoining of the exhibition, I found the newly restored Ottilie portrait in the 4th or 5th room and took a few minutes to examine and photograph the work. We decided to continue through the exhibition, and before long found the lithograph of Pastor Matthias Thiel, as I had seen it in the National Museum of Art four years before. Scanning the room, I came across another, unknown to me at that juncture, a second lithograph entitled, the Flying Hollander.

Rundale portrait exhibition, 2009

And on an adjacent wall two more labeling oil paintings of an unnamed gentleman and an unnamed lady. I had no previous knowledge of the existence of the last three, and, of course, was surprised and pleased to discover them. The known (to me) works of Johann Karl Ludwig Maddaus were multiplying before my eyes!

We followed our trip to Rundale with day trips to Tirza (my first visit there) and Paistu (my second) and with each, the pastor and congregation celebrated the return of the artist. I couldn't help but feel honored on each occasion, although all I had done was make the trip. The reverence for the artist, for any artist, is a unique and palpable feeling that I had not considered much before and I find it endearing in its sentiment. No matter who the artist is or how he/she leads his/her life, his/her lasting work can be enjoyed and celebrated long after he/she is gone. And Beth and I were a party to this uplifting sentiment on both occasions.

The white and red-roofed steeple of Tirza Evangelical Lutheran Church extends high up on the hill overlooking the small village and can be seen from quite a distance from some vantage-points. Pastor Valdis serves two congregations part-time and also runs a school for orphan children, some distance to the south of the church. He is effusive, enthusiastic and out-going, and always seems to be thinking two or three steps ahead of where he is, while somehow staying in the present. Pastor Valdis and a few families arranged a special Saturday service for the occasion and he asked me to speak about my ancestry. I was then anointed, as though I were the artist's surrogate, and the painting was blessed.

We were led out the rear of the church onto the back lawn where the congregation had arranged a beautiful meal full of finger rolls, fruits and fresh local vegetables. Pastor Valdis and one woman who spoke English interpreted for us, as we enjoyed a summer's afternoon in the Latvian countryside.

The Tirza church had an interesting and difficult history from its origins to the late-16th century, with the current structure's foundation laid in 1823. The painting, "Christ in the Garden of Gethsemane," was one of Johann Maddaus' earlier altar paintings, dating to 1843. Soviet occupation in the 20th century was characterized by unusually high taxes placed on the congregation, as a way of extracting wealth from the congregation, and ultimately the church became a Soviet storage facility, falling to disrepair.

Tirza Lutheran Church

Renovation of the church began shortly after re-independence in 1992, and we learned from our female interpreter that her husband, Nils, Eižens Upmanis' friend, had helped coordinate the renovation effort. Later at their country house, which they also renovated in period style, we learned more about the occupation, the church and the community and were given a book which outlined the entire history of the church, also part of Nils' effort in reestablishing the church.

After a night in a rustic hotel near Tirza we traveled to Paistu, Estonia for a Sunday service at Mary's Church. This time, our interpreter was the young adult daughter of a member of the congregation, who traveled from Tallinn, the capital, for the occasion. She was 5 or 6 months pregnant at the time and glowing as pregnant women often are. We had a similar experience in the service to my last visit, following the liturgy in Estonian much in the same order as we knew it would be in an American Lutheran church. And again, we were treated to a small gathering and meal after the service. Nothing in my experience quite equates with the hospitality I have experienced in these small Baltic church communities.

Before heading back to Riga, we satisfied my curiosity in all things related to Nordic skiing, by spending a night in Otepää, Estonia, a regular stop on the World Cup Nordic skiing schedule each year. I ran one of the loops that in winter would be filled with skiers, and marveled at the paved roller-ski training loops which crisscrossed the area. No wonder Olympic champions Andrus Veerpalu and Jaak Mae trained here.

For this trip we had a postlude planned, that is, a few days in Sweden. Beth's daughter Sara, who was serving in the Peace Corps in Macedonia at the time, took some time off and met us in Stockholm and from there we headed for the Silja Lake area of central Sweden. The setting was as scenic and relaxing as the Baltic countryside, with attractions of its own and I took the opportunity to reflect and savor my time in Latvia and Estonia, even as Beth and Sara searched for authentic Dala horses outside of Mora.

Chapter Ten

Johann Karl Ludwig Maddaus
(1820-1878)

JKLM self-portrait

Little knowledge or documentation of the life of our great, great grandfather, Johann Karl Ludwig Maddaus, made its way to America with the emigration of our great grandfather Oscar Wilhelm Maddaus and his family from Riga in the late 19th century. We can only speculate how the artist and his work became obscured from family recollection. Oscar Wilhelm lived only 13 years from his second and final move from Riga to Brooklyn, before his accidental death in 1896. His wife Augusta, may have had limited knowledge of her husband's family—her family was a mix of Latvian and German households—whereas her father-in-law was patriarch of a firmly German merchant-class family. Oscar's children—3 boys and 3 girls—ranged in age of 19 to 6 at the time of his death and the older ones were thrust into the role of providing for their mother and younger siblings. Most had heard some stories about their grandfather, but only two had been born at the time of his death in 1878.

Johann was born February 21, 1820 in Hamburg, an independent city recovering from the Napoleonic occupation of the previous decade. His parents were Georg and Henriette Dede Maddaus, and he had two younger siblings, Johanne and Ludwig. Johann's father was listed as a painter in one public record, but little is known of his work. Georg died in 1823, leaving his wife with the 3 young children.

Henriette Dede Maddaus moved after her second marriage to a merchant named Johann Burghausen to his home in Frosche, near Magdeberg, a few years after Johann's father's death. Young Johann was likely educated in Hamburg--though not necessarily—but in any event he followed the route to Riga that many Hamburg and Magdeburg merchants and artisans had taken since the beginning of Hanseatic League in the 13th century. He certainly may have been influenced by the presence of former Magdeberg composer Richard Wagner in Riga in the late 1830s. Both cities had connections to the German mercantile and cultural communities in Riga. In any case, he seems to have arrived in Riga in 1840 and lived there until his death in 1878. Our family oral history suggests that Johann moved to Riga to avoid conscription in the Prussian Army. This would be true if he was considered a citizen of Magdeberg, not Hamburg, his place of birth, as Hamburg was independent of Prussia in the late 1830s.

Johann Karl Ludwig Maddaus is how he is listed in Dr. Wilhelm Neumann's "Lexikon Baltischer Kunstler," the 19th Century Baltic artist directory, published in Riga in 1908, though he is referred to as Johann Ludwig Karl and just Ludwig in a variety of sources. He was a portrait artist and drawing teacher at the No. 2 Riga Kreisschule (school district) from the early 1840s until July of 1877. He is known for portraits in lithograph and oil and produced a number of altar paintings for churches in 19th century Livland, territory now known as northern Latvia and southern Estonia. The altar paintings are interesting in that it is apparent that he was asked to reproduce work of the great masters; two of his most significant pieces (Mary's Church in Paistu Estonia and Garkalne Lutheran Church) are based on the work of 17th century Dutch artist Peter Paul Rubens and Leonardo daVinci, respectively. Altar paintings were also completed for churches in Carnikava, Jaunpiebalga, Tirza and Turaida.

Johann's oil portraits and altar paintings reflect the "Biedermeier" style of mid-19th century Europe. While not a formally classified style of art, Biedermeier reflected a general characteristic in the fields of literature, music, the visual arts and interior design relative to the growing middle-class sensibilities of the age. A pair of his portraits are described as depictions of middle-class figures reduced in "informal, laid-back images—a cozy, chubby lady holds a kerchief while a respectable gentleman reclines in a chair in somewhat relaxed posture."

His altar paintings were copies of works of some of the great artists of Western Europe, most notably Peter Paul Rubens and Leonardo da Vinci. His work was notable for its faith to the original, his life-like human figures and the reasonable price he charged for their production. "Art History of Latvia, Volume III" notes that when he "had made the altarpieces The Descent from the Cross (after Peter Paul Rubens) and The Last Supper (after Leonardo da Vinci) for Jaunpiebalga Church in 1850, pastor Karl Ludwig Kaehlbrandt (1803–1888) and congregation superior, Baron Alexander von Meyendorff (1802–1872) placed a recommendation in the newspaper "Rigasche Zeitung" for other commissioners, informing that the artist had realised these works for a very moderate price." And when a work destined for Paistu, Estonia was displayed in Riga's St. John's Church in 1852, the critical summation in "In Land" points out "the portrayal of suffering in the Savior's face, the expression of mourning among women at the foot of the cross, has something moving, the colors are alive, the garments they are painstakingly painted and the whole thing has pleasantly reminded us of the original," Ruben's "The Crucifixion of Christ." The various known altar paintings are discussed individually later in this book.

Johann looked for an ever-expanding range of media to express his artistry and delved into the early development of photography. According to Art Historian Inta Pujate,

> It seems he got skills in photography in the studio of Johann Everhard Feilner who arrived from Bremen in Riga and opened a studio here in August 1852. When Feilner went back Maddaus started to take photographs in Feilner's previous studio near a Rathause in March 1853. After five months he moved the studio to his flat in Haus Losch (now Kungu un Peldu ielas), then in August 1857 he opened studio at Haus of Merchant Schulz (now Kaļķu iela). The last information about Maddaus as photographer I found in 1861 – he has taken a photo of Saengerfestballe in Riga (an important event – the first German Song Festival in Latvia) at July.
>
> Maddaus was well-known at his time, he often didn't mention an address of his studio in the advertisings. He made daguerreotypes, copies on a paper and in the middle of fifties started to take stereoscopic photographs.....he was interested in photography and tried to find new possibilities to interest other people in this field as well in his activities. Maybe he was the first at Riga who exhibited stereoscopic tinted views. So, his investment in the history of photography of the 19th century in Latvia is quite important.

One summer Johann put on an exhibition of his photos of various sites he'd visited throughout Western Europe including present-day Switzerland, France and Germany. Income from his portrait and altar painting work certainly had given him the income to make his travels possible, as salary from his teaching position would not have supported such opportunities otherwise.

Johann was married only once, according 19th century church records. His marriage to Adele Dorothea Ernestine Gertrud Zirckmann was recorded in the Rigas Doma (Riga Dome Church) in 1842. Her name appears in various forms in records of her birth (Dorothea Adela Ernestine Gertrud, born Sept. 9, 1823 in Riga) and the births of her and Johann's 8 children, although she seems to have been known as Adele. The children were Alexander Albert (Dec. 1843), Oscar Wilhelm (our great grandfather, born 1845), Ottilie Angelina Emilie (Oct. 1847), Johanna Adele (May 1850, died as an infant), Johanna Elvira Adele (Oct 1851), August Ludwig (Feb. 1854), Emma Gertrud (Feb. 1857) and Eugen Adolph Wilhelm (Oct. 1858). Emma and Eugen both died in 1860. Alexander, Oscar and Ottilie were baptized in the Rigas Doma, after which the family changed allegiance and had the others baptized in the St. Peter's Church. Both are iconic churches on the Riga skyline.

Adele was the daughter of Abraham Diedrich and Agathe Mariana (Schultz) Zirckmann. Abraham was born in Kurland, what is now known as Kurzeme, in western Latvia. That she was known as Adele is a guess on my part, but two of her grandchildren were so named. She died in Riga on December 8, 1908, thirty years after her husband. She apparently returned to the Rigas Doma congregation after his death and was involved in the Riga cultural community.

It was Adele's donation of the self-portrait of Johann and portrait of Ottilie to the new art museum which landed Johann in Neumann's register, and those two portraits along with a lithograph remain in the Latvian National Art Museum collection. Without these donations and the register listing, the artist's life might have been totally blotted out by World War II and the ensuing Soviet occupation. As it stands, his stature as an artist is limited by this 'dark side' of Baltic German art history, prior to the 20th century. He was more of a craftsman or artisan than a creative artist and his work reflects this modest workmanship.

Little is known of Johann and Adele's children, other than what I have unearthed about our great grandfather, Oscar Wilhelm.

Alexander, the oldest, died in 1915 at the age of 72, apparently the last Maddaus to live in Riga. Alexander may have been a teacher, like his father, and he seems to have remained close to his mother.

Oscar Wilhelm immigrated to Brooklyn, NY sometime before 1870, had a first wife, Margaret Brown, and three children, who died in the influenza epidemic of the winter of 1872-3. He then wrote to our great grandmother, Augusta Dorothea Rathminder, and she agreed to travel to America from Riga to be his (2nd) wife. Oscar followed his father's trade, working primarily in woodcut art for advertising and catalog businesses, and was also an accomplished musician with a well-known chamber group. He died in 1896, survived by Augusta and 6 teenaged children. Augusta lived with three of them in various Brooklyn apartments until her death in 1937.

Ottilie, who was depicted in one of her father's portraits, was a pianist and world traveler, popping up at a finishing school in Illinois and on passenger lists bound for England and France. She lived out her later adult life in Riga, alternately working as an English teacher and piano/keyboards instructor and dying there in 1913.

Johanna Elvira Adele is linked in historical records with her younger brother August Ludwig as they were accompanied by their mother to Hamburg in the 1860s to further their education, but additional detail of Johanna is unknown. August rose to become director of a factory in Voroshilovo (Smolensk province) in present-day Russia. He married twice. His first wife Ida, died in childbirth with the delivery of their daughter Adela in 1880. He and his second wife, Vera Schurawoff, had two children-- Eugen (1882) and Arnna (1884).

Johann, Adele, Alexander Albert, August and his second wife, Vera are all buried in the family plot in Lielie Kapi (The Great Cemetery) in Riga.

While Johann established himself in Riga, and his surviving progeny are located in America, it's interesting to note that Johann's sister's family also traveled far from Hamburg and Magdeburg. Johanne's daughters moved to Peru where Adolphina met and married a Scot named Robert Reid. Their progeny spread across the globe to England, New Zealand and Canada.

Chapter Eleven

The Artwork of Johann Karl Ludwig Maddaus
++++++++++++++++++++

The following are the documented works of Johann Maddaus, known as of the date of this publication. Included are images of a selection of his works in oil, lithograph and water color including altar paintings he produced. The information varies, depending on additional sources I have found. Included are photos of those I have been lucky enough to see first-hand.

While Johann was active in landscape and portrait photography during the 1850s and 1860s, no known examples of this photography work are extant.

Self-Portrait

Oil on cardboard
Oval 30 x 24.5 cm
Date: Unknown
Restored 2012
Collection of the Latvian National Museum of Art
Riga, Latvia

JKLM Self-Portrait restoration

Johann's Self-Portrait was donated by his widow to the Latvian National Museum of Art sometime before her death, and, indeed, before the official opening of the Museum. It is an oval oil painting on cardboard in a vertical orientation, with a gold frame. The painting was restored in 2012-3 and the frame was to be restored to its original gold from the black overcoat that was applied at some point in its 100+ year life. On further review by restoration experts, the frame was not restored.

Portrait of Ottilie Maddaus

Oil on cardboard
c. 1870
Restored 2008 (?)
62 x 51 cm (oval)
Collection of the Latvian National Museum of Art
Riga, Latvia

Portrait of Ottilie Maddaus, after restoration

Johann Maddaus had two daughters reach adulthood, Ottilie, born 1847, and Johanna, born 1851. Ottilie traveled extensively, including sojourns to America and England, but lived most her life in Riga where she gave private lessons in both English and piano. According to Inta Pujate's "Portrets Latvija 19.gadsimts" ("19th Century Latvian Portraits"), Johanna lived for a while in Minsk, and in May 1883 she returned to Riga and ran a school.

While it is not certain, given the approximate age of the painting and "the age of the depicted person, suggests that the artist portrayed his daughter Ottilie here."

The painting was restored sometime between 2005 and 2009 and included in the 19th Century Latvian Portraits exhibition at Rundale Palace in the summer of 2009.

Portrait of Pastor Matthias Thiel

1843
Lithograph on paper
41.7 x 33 cm
Collection of Latvian National Museum of Art
Riga, Latvia

Portrait of Pastor Matthias Thiel

Matthias Thiel was the son of Franz Johann Thiel, businessman and brewer, and Anna Dorothea (Ehlers) Thiel, a pastor and social worker. Matthias attended the cathedral school (Domschule) and studied at Jena in Thuringia (central Germany) and was then tutor in Courland (Western Latvia). In 1800, he returned to Riga and was active as in both spiritual and legal affairs, later becoming Superintendent and head pastor of St. Peter's church, member of several societies, and writing theological and historical essays. In 1801, he married to Agnes Juliana Gottlieb von Heyking.

Johann Maddaus was connected with St. Peter's Church for much of his life and agreed to produce Thiel's portrait in lithograph sometime in the year prior to the pastor's death.

The lithograph was included in the 19th Century Latvian Portraits exhibition at Rundale Palace in 2009 and detailed in Inta Pujate's publication "Latvija Portrets 19.gadsimts."

Portrait of Actor Karl Gunther in the Lead Role in Richard Wagner Opera "The Flying Dutchman"
(German: *Der fliegende Holländer*)

1842 (?)
Lithograph on Paper
56.3 x 32.7 cm
Collection of Museum of the History of Riga and Navigation
Riga, Latvia

The Flying Dutchman

One of Johann Maddaus' earliest known works was the lithograph of Carl Gunther in the role of The Flying Dutchman in the Wagner opera of the same name.

Wagner himself had moved to Riga (then part of the Russian Empire) in 1837 amidst serious financial and romantic difficulties.

Although reunited with his love Minna, his troubles continued in Riga and they departed for London in 1839 to avoid creditors. As the story goes, the sea voyage to London served as inspiration for "Der Fliegende Holländer" ("The Flying Dutchman"). Whether this is true was cast in doubt when Wagner acknowledged he had taken the story from a Heinrich Henne work, although it certainly could have been a combination of inspirational factors. The work is regarded as the beginning of the mature canon of the composer.

Wagner premiered the opera in Dresden, in January 1843 and later that same year, Johann Karl Ludwig Maddaus completed the lithograph to coincide with a Riga performance. Maddaus and Wagner shared a connection in that they both came to Riga after some time in Magdeburg and indeed, Maddaus' move to Riga followed Wagner and many others. Our family connection with the opera was continued with the naming of Johann's granddaughter Senta, after the heroine of the opera.

The lithograph was included in the 19th Century Latvian Portraits exhibition at Rundale Palace in 2009 and detailed in Inta Pujate's publication "Latvija Portrets 19.gadsimts."

Portrait of a Man

Oil on Canvas
46 x 37.5 cm

Portrait of a Woman

Oil on canvas
46 x 38 cm
Jurmala City Museum
Jurmala. Latvia

Two of the earliest oil paintings by Johann Maddaus, "The Portrait of a Man" and "The Portrait of a Woman", represent the artist's entry into commercial oil portraiture and led to his later work in church alter paintings.

The unknown gentleman seated formally against a barren background with his hand in his jacket, possibly after the example by Napoleon, is presented in the Biedermeier style that was popular in mid-century Europe. Although not documented as such, the companion portrait is believed to be the wife of the gentleman.

The portraits were part of a significant donation to the Jurmala City Museum by the Pormanis Family when the Museum was established in 1962.

The portraits were included in the 19th Century Latvian Portraits exhibition at Rundale Palace in 2009 and detailed in Inta Pujate's publication "Latvija Portrets 19.gadsimts." A photo from that exhibit is found in Chapter 9.

Võnnu Church
(Cesis Church)

1869
Watercolor on paper
23.1 x 30.6 cm (oval)
Art Museum of Estonia
Tallinn, Estonia

Võnnu Church

An internet search led to the discovery of this small watercolor in the collection of the Estonian national museum. It is the only known work of the artist in this medium.

The scene is a long view of the city of Võnnu (present-day Cesis) and it's iconic St. John's Church. References in the Estonian museum confuse the setting with Valmeira, but the church is clearly St. John's in Cesis.

Kristus ristil
(Christ on the Cross)

Altar painting in oil on canvas
134 x 268 cm
1852
Paistu Maarja kogudus (Mary's Church)
Paistu, Estonia

Christ on the Cross, Mary's Church altar painting, Paistu, Estonia

Paistu sits at the highpoint in farmland 12 kilometers south of the city of Viljandi in Viljandi County (Viljandimaa), a south-central municipality of Estonia bordering Latvia. The village of 350 residents is part of Viljandi Parish and is 40 kilometers from the border.

The stone structure, formally known as the Church of St. Mary the Virgin (Paistu Puha Neitsi kirik), dates to the 4th quarter of the 13th century and was first mentioned in historical records in 1329 in connection with a raid by Lithuanians. Mary's church has weathered both war and natural disasters over its seven centuries in existence. The tower, mentioned as early as 1668, was destroyed during the Great Northern War of the early 18th century and the rebuilt tower was torched by lightning in 1817 all but destroying the church and its organ. The existing interior was completed mainly between 1852 and 1853, at which time the pulpit, altar and organ were installed. It was during this restoration that the Maddaus altar painting was commissioned and installed.

A wind storm severely damaged the recently installed roof of the church in 2003 largely due to a design flaw in the installation. Additional damage to the church resulted in another round of repairs over the next two years. The altar painting was also restored during this period.

The church and a number of the 'mobile memorials' including the painting, the wooden altar, chandeliers and the tower clock, are all listed in the Estonian National Register of Cultural Monuments. The description of the painting, "Kolgata" Register No. 19843, translates roughly as follows:

> The center of the painting is the Crucifixion, depicted by the artist as a muscular, coarse male figure, with his chest stretched forward, his head tilted to his left shoulder, his eyes half closed. The hands are nailed to the cross-tree relatively close together, the feet-wide, the right foot on the top. The white thread belt forms a lush drape, the ends of which flutter on the right hip. A name tag with inverted ends above the head of the crucifixion in three languages (with Joh 19, 20: Jesus of Nazareth, King of the Jews): the first two lines in Hebrew, the next three lines in Greek (Iηςους ὁ ὁ Βασιλευς των.), the bottom three lines in Latin (IESUS NAZARENUS REX IUDEORUM.).
>
> A group of people has been assembled around the crusade. A woman in a red coat on the left side of the foreground and an elderly woman with a grey headscarf, her arms raised to her chest,

is painted in a semi-turning turn towards the cross. A young, dark-haired woman, Mary Magdalene, crouched in front of the crucifixion, is a red, wide-necked tunic that leaves her shoulders bare; her knees are covered by a green drape. Her lowered head is in profile to the left, her folded hands in her lap. Behind the cross to the right is a young man in red robes… leaning his head to one side…. a fluttering purple-colored drape in his arms. The half-figure of a grey-bearded man with a red turban under the end of the drapery in the background, a grey female figure in the shadow of his shoulder, the head and neck of a grey horse. On the right side of the picture, behind Mary Magdalene, is a bearded old man with a grey-blue headgear, with a shuddering look at the Crucifixion (Nicodemus?). In the dark sky, a bright dash of light to the left of the crucifixion, the houses of Jerusalem visible in the gasp of the horizon. In the foreground, on the ground, little grass, three skulls, and a tibia bone.

Mary Magdalene depicted in Kristus ristil

The new altar is made from 310 rubles from the organist Normann's drawing. There was no altar picture before 1853. Getting the current altar picture was the work of Karl Maurach, a homeschool teacher for the Cumming family of a rich English merchant in Riga. The eldest, lively daughter was so engaged by Maurach's religious lessons that she prevailed on her father to commission the altar painting for his chosen church. For this purpose, the other siblings also donated sums of pocket money. The father, seeing the children's enthusiasm, gave a greater sum. The young girl's heart did not come true to her grief. She died early; his father remained poor afterwards.

The Church of Paistu, however, received a prized altar image produced by someone named Maddaus … The picture depicts the most gripping moment of the Kolgata event, when Jesus' head fell down after saying "Finished!". The disciple of love stretches out his hands to fight back death, Mary Magdalene is crushed, and Jesus' mother puts her hands on the heart from which the sword of pain penetrates. Away from several other spectators, friends of the Son of God. Above, the clouds are thickening. Through the clouds, only half of the sun appears, which must mean a struggle between life and death, the darkness of the world and the light of life.

The idea in itself is beautiful, though, from the artistic side, the painting leaves a little to be desired for Maurach's decision. A local farmer, Hendrik Ainson of nearby Holstre at his own expense brought the painting from Riga with his horses and wagon. Unfortunately, the transporter was struck by a serious accident: after a few days his barn burned to the ground. Both horses were killed in the fire, but the painting was delivered.

https://register.muinas.ee/public.php?menuID=monument&action=view&id=19843

The tragic ending of both the horses and the young girl referenced in 'Maurach's decision' draw a direct line from the sacrificial death of Christ to the painting's commission, the connection deepening its impact. It is probably Johann Maddaus' finest work, a testament to his ability to follow the European masters like Peter Paul Rubens, whose work he used as a model in this case.

Christ on the Cross

Altar painting in oil
Carnikavas baznica (Carnikava Lutheran Church)
Carnikava, Latvia

Carnikava is located just 25 km northeast of the Riga at the mouth of the Gauja River. The municipality borders Adazi to the south and includes significant frontage on the Baltic Sea. Early mention of Carnikava as a Livonian fishing center dates to 1211. The church site is located on the northeast bank of the Gauja in the hamlet of Siguli, less than 5k from its mouth.

In Volume One of his four-volume "Lutheran Churches of Latvia," published in 2005, Vitolds Mašnovskis notes:

> Local peasants financed and built the first wooden church at Carnikava in 1643. In the 1720s the owner of the Carnikava estate, G. von Mengden, had a new wooden church built on the site. After his death in 1726, Mengden's widow, D. S. von Mengden nee Rosen, oversaw the construction of the church, which was completed in 1728. In 1851, with financial support from P. Pander (the owner of the Carnikava estate), the congregation expanded the church to seat 180 and added a steeple to it.

Mašnovskis suggests the expansion included the addition of Maddaus' altar painting.

> The 1851 painting "Christ on the Cross" (in Latvian, 'Kristus pie krusta') by J.K.L. Maddaus (1820-1878), who emigrated to Latvia from Hamburg in 1840, was located between two Corinthian columns on the level of the two-level altar retable, which dated from the 1720s.

It was a review of Mašnovskis work in the online blog Latvians Online which first brought his work to my attention, and also alerted me to multiple altar paintings by our artist ancestor still in existence in Latvia. Ironically, this is one which has been in storage for a number of years and I have only seen a black and white photo of it.

The interior of the church building would suffer damage during World War I and the exterior in World War II, but the congregation was able to restore the damage each time. Attendance and membership dwindled until the last service in 1954 and the building was repurposed by the Soviets—as many churches were—in this case to an electrical fuse box factory.

The church was returned to the congregation in 1992, unusable and neglected until a fundraising campaign, coordinated by the nearby Baltezers Lutheran Church under the umbrella of the Adazi Parish and with Cultural Ministry support, resulted in a restoration effort in the late 2000s and early 2010s.

Tragically, with restoration close at hand, the church building fell prey to mindless arson in December 2017 and burnt to the ground. At the time of the fire, the church was considered one of the oldest wooden churches of its kind on the Vidzeme coast. Services had been planned in the restored building for when Latvia celebrated its 100th anniversary in 2018.

Pastor Ivars broke the sad news of the fire at worship on the morning of December 10, 2017 with the message "this is not just a loss to the Parish of Carnikava church but it's a loss to the whole historical heritage of Latvia and Europe." A renewed effort to rebuild is in process at this writing, but the timetable and support remains in doubt. Fortunately, the painting and other interior pieces still survive.

In recent months the congregation has met in a 'boathouse' closer to the center of Carnikava and the parish announced its intention to rebuild the child on the same plot of land.

The Last Supper

Altar painting in oil
60 x 90 cm
Garkalnes Evangeliski luteriska baznica (Garkalne Lutheran Church)
Garkalne, Latvia

The Last Supper, Garkalnes Lutheran Church altar painting

Garkalne borders Adazi and the church is part of the Adazi Parish. Construction of the small white church nestled in the pines began in March 1848 and was completed by July of that year. The building was used as a storehouse during WWII and the congregation finally regained the use of it in 1991 after which restoration of the church foundation, steeple and interior was completed.

Mašnovskis' description of the altar retable indicates:

> On the lower section is the painting "The Last Supper" by Hamburg artist J.K.L. Maddaus (1820-1878), who also painted the Tirza and Carnikava altar paintings. The signature on the reverse of the painting reads: L. Maddaus d: 20 Juli 1848.

While the Maddaus rendition of The Last Supper includes all the same characters in the same order as the da Vinci masterpiece, certain differences are apparent when the two works are compared side-to-side.

The copy features greater height versus its width and Maddaus uses the additional area to expand the ceiling. It gives more emphasis to the perspective of the room but, unfortunately, takes attention from the featured event and its principal. The face of Christ in this copy is slightly below the center of the painting whereas his face is intentionally in the center of da Vinci's work.

In addition, the copy provides no contrast on the side walls where the master has a series of 4 tapestries hung on either side. Maddaus frames the total of 8 spaces but colors the walls, framing and space with the same dark green hue. The background windows approximate the same serene scene.

While the characters are more or less in the same order and with the same positioning, ten of the twelve are dressed in different colored attire than the original. Only Jesus and the apostle seated next to him, generally identified as James the Greater, feature the same color robes. Saint Thomas the Doubter's head only appears between the two, but the all others vary from the original.

One other difference is noted in the color of one apostle's hair. In the original, Saint Simon the Zealot—at the far right—has reddish brown hair and beard but Maddaus has clearly chosen grey for this solitary change. This aligns with one copy of the original made by Giampietrino, one of da Vinci's students, which suggests greyer facial hair for Simon.

Other minor differences may be noted in the tableware, for instance where the original includes a bowl and plate in front of Jesus, Maddaus omits the bowl. Table legs, feet and floor all appear more or less the same in both versions, although Maddaus seems to emphasize the dimensions of the flooring more than the original.

We can only speculate on the method the artist used to recreate the work, as it is unknown whether he had seen the original, worked from another copy or notes made by another. The dimensions of the painting likely came from the requirements of the church. The original work of da Vinci is about 15' by 29' (460cm by 880cm) or almost a ratio of 1:2, whereas the much smaller Maddaus copy (approximately 24" by 32" or 60 cm by 90 cm) is at a ratio of 3:4. The color choices were probably a question of artistic interpretation. As there are currently known copies of da Vinci's work painted by his students in the early 16th century, and now located in London, Belgium and Switzerland, it's conceivable that variations of these copies made their way to Hamburg, Maddaus' hometown, or Riga.

Overall, Maddaus' copy of da Vinci's masterpiece serves the purpose intended, that of depicting the holy event artistically. Certainly, the average observer in 1848 when it was completed, or today for that matter, would know the work as The Last Supper, and its place behind the altar directly below an unattributed painting titled "Christ on the Cross" would signify the importance of the image.

Christ on the Cross

Altar painting in oil
Svētā Toma evanģēliski luteriskā baznīca (St. Thomas Church)
Jaunpiebalga, Latvia

Jaunpiebalga is located about 160 kilometers east of Riga in the heart of the Piebalga region of Vidzeme. Our Rathminder ancestors hailed from Vecpiebalga, just 20 km to the west.

The construction of a wooden church in Jaunpiebalga with the financial help of the wife of Field Marshall Boris Sheremetyev was completed in 1723 but it succumbed to fire in 1804 during the building of the existing masonry church.

Our ancestor's artistic contributions to the church came in 1850. As noted in "Art History of Latvia, Volume III, Part 2:"

> When Johann Karl Ludwig Maddaus (1820-1878) had made the altarpieces *The Descent from the Cross* (after Peter Paul Rubens) and *The Last Supper* (after Leonardi da Vinci) for Jaunpiebalga Church in 1850, pastor Karl Ludwig Kaehlbrandt (1803-1888) and congregation superior, Baron Alexander von Mayenhoff (1802-1872) placed a recommendation in the newspaper *Rigasche Zeitung* for other commissioners, informing that the artist had realized these works for a very moderate price.

The recommendation surely could not have done anything but enhance the marketability of Maddaus' work.

Mašnovskis makes no mention of Maddaus or the da Vinci reproduction in the church in his 4-volume encyclopedia of Latvia churches. He does include a photo of the altar painting *Christ on the Cross* but the detail of this work bears little resemblance to the Rubens work which Maddaus faithfully copied for the Paistu church in Estonia.

So, what happened to the 1850 paintings? The answer is unclear, but according to some sources one or both may have been stolen during

Soviet Times when the church fell into disrepair. In fact, the roof, ceiling and interior walls were damaged during World War II. By 2004, the structure had been renovated enough for the congregation to celebrate its 200th anniversary.

Jesus in the Garden of Gethsemane

Altar painting in oil
Tirza Evanģēliski luteriskā baznīca (Tirza Lutheran Church)
Tirza, Latvia

Jesus in the Garden of Gethsemane, Tirza altar painting

Another 30 km east of Jaunpiebalga is the village of Tirza and its interesting Lutheran Church. The construction of the first church here began in 1589 and stood until is was plundered and burned down by Count Sheremetyev's army in 1702. Various iterations followed until the current masonry church was built nearby and dedicated in 1826.

Mašnovskis notes the church is "a rectangular stone and brick masonry construction built in the Late Neo-Classicism style" and has "a tall, two-stepped polygonal steeple and a portico consisting of a triangular pediment supported by four Ionic columns". Situated on the top of a hill overlooking the adjacent farmland, the church is impressive in its perspective if not of imposing size.

Mašnovskis outlines briefly in his encyclopedia the source of the altar painting:

> The Neo-Classicism style altar was made in 1826. It consists of two pairs of Corinthian columns on his bases supporting a thick dentil-decorated entablature. On the retable is the painting *"Christ in the Garden of Gethsemane"* (1843) by Johann Karl Ludwig Maddaus (1820-1878) of Hamburg.

The dating on this painting places it among the earliest altar paintings produced by the artist, and not long after his arrival in Riga. No mention of a source for this work is evident, and although Maddaus was known to have painted copies of the work of Rubens, this one in particular bears little resemblance to work of the Dutch artist. Closest in content and layout is the El Greco work "Christ on the mount of Olives" but Maddaus varies dramatically in the stylistically. The painting demonstrates Maddaus' early skills and provides a presages the young artist's future work.

With apostles Peter and James and John huddled sleeping together in the foreground, Jesus sits in prayerful pose in the center surrounded by three angels close by and bright glow of the heavens ringed by dark clouds behind him. A golden cup rests before Christ and as Mark 14: 36 tells us, Jesus prays: "And he said, Abba, Father, all things are possible unto thee; take away this cup from me: nevertheless not what I will, but what thou wilt," (KJV) and he prepares for the moment of betrayal by Judas.

The painting transmits little of the 'agony of the garden' as the scene is often described, but rather a faithful submission and resignation to the role which Christ knew was his fate. That he is surrounded by heavenly bodies sanctifies the event and provides the viewer with a sense of both alarm and comfort in the events to follow, in spite of the inability of the disciples to be alert to them.

As with many churches during Soviet times, Tirza Lutheran Church was subjected to misuse and the congregation discouraged by a variety of means. Mašnovskis notes in Tirza's case 'an unusually high tax burden forced the congregation to leave the church in 1987,' but returned in 1989. The building was used for storage over a period of years. Significant renovations began in 1992 culminating in completion in time for the church's 180th anniversary celebration in August, 2006. The final year represented a concerted effort led by architects Ilmars Dirveiks and Ilze Janele, coordinator Nils Treijs and civil engineer Modris Sergejevs, along with the spiritual leadership of pastor Valdis Strazdins. Nils Treijs performed double-duty in editing a church history for the occasion, entitled "Tirzas baznica un draudze Laikmeta Griezos, 1429-2006."

Christ on the Cross

Altar painting in oil
53 x 35 cm
Turaidas evaņģēliski luteriskā baznīca (Turaida Lutheran Church)
Turaida, Latvia

Turaida Lutheran Church

This version of "Christ on the Cross," or "Golgotha," is a departure from Johann Maddaus' other altar paintings due to the overall dark quality of the work. Dated 1843, the same year "Jesus in the Garden of Gethsemane" was produced for the Tirza church, the painting features Christ nailed to the cross covered around the waist only by white swaddling robes the ends unfurled at either side. The top of the cross in adorned with the Pontius Pilate's notice in Latin, "INRI," from the phrase 'Iesus Nazerenus Rex Iudaeorum,' meaning Jesus of Nazareth, King of the Jews.

The relative brightness of figure of the Christ, his white 'attire,' and the notice are contrasted by the cross, a skull and various bones in the foreground and a vague depiction of Calvary Hill in the background, all in darker 'brownish' hues. On my visit to the church it seemed apparent that the painting needed some restoration as the surface bore signs of aging.

The present, small (capacity 100) wooden church was constructed using funds from local farmers in 1750-51 and is the third to be built on the site. The church tower dates to some 58 years later and was funded by the owner of the Turaida estate. The congregation was forced to relinquish the church in 1965 and fortunately it was given to the Turaida Museum Reserve with encompasses Turaida Castle—one of the most dramatic landmarks in Latvia due to its promontory overlooking the Gauja River across the valley from the small resort city of Sigulda—the church, the Turaida Estate and the surrounding grounds.

Mašnovskis notes that

> The altar painting "Golgotha" 953 x 35 cm), made by Hamburg artist J.K.L. Maddaus in 1843, is that the center of the simple altar retable. Volutes form the retable frontispiece and wings. The "Golgotha" painting was on the altar until 1926, when it was replaced with a painting titled "Christ in the Garden of Gethsemane" (102 x 73 cm), donated by the Sauer family. "Golgotha" was put back on the retable when the Sigulda local history museum took over the church.

The painting would be the most viewed of Maddaus' works as the Turaida Museum Reserve is among the most visited tourist attractions in Latvia, second only to the Latvian National Museum of Art in Riga. Recent annual visit counts exceed 260,000 people.

Recent research puts the authorship in doubt and although the inscription on the back of the painting reads "L. Maddan/d .20 Juli 1843." The Turaida Museum Reserve has indicted that during restoration by the National Museum of Art, art scientists were not convinced of the authorship. 'Archaetonically artistic research' of the Turaida Church performed by Intarsia Ltd. in 2006 suggest the time of the painting is 17th century or early 18th century. According to Anna Jurkāne of the Museum Reserve:

The art scientist Ojārs Spārītis, whose article entitled "The Church of Turaida and the Tradition of the Construction of Lutheran Churches in Vidzeme," published in 2001 in the book issued by the Turaida Museum Reserve "The Turaida Church 1750 – 2000/ compiled by L. Kreišmane" is sure that the painting was created in the 17th century.

Spārītis is former Latvian Minister of Culture, the current President of the Latvian Academy of Sciences and Director of the Doctoral Program of the Latvian Academy of Art. He is a prolific author of works relating to art and the arts.

Authorship of the Turaida Church altar painting remains unknown as well as the reason for the inscription on the back identifying our ancestor, although it might suggest his contribution to some restoration work needed at the time of the dating.

Chapter Twelve

Latvia - February 2010

My return to Vecpiebalga for the third time developed over a series of emails with English teachers at the Vecpiebalga Vidusskola (Secondary School), the establishment of a collaborative online exchange between my 9th grade English students and 12th 'klase' English students in Vecpiebalga and a suggestion by my wife that I might travel to Latvia during her visit with her daughter, who is serving in the Peace Corps in Macedonia. I jump at this opportunity and I am treated as I imagine a foreign dignitary might be. I am, after all, the descendant of the family of Andžs Rātminders, the longest serving educator in Latvian history, and a beloved son of Vecpiebalga.

My contacts arrange for me to stay with Maris and Agita, who both teach physical education in the school and Maris is charged with giving me a tour of the Nordic ski trails around Alauksts Lake—15 kilometers—with one of his friends and a student who is one of their top skiers serving as escorts. The route is used for the annual Apkārt Alaukstam (Around Alauksts) ski race on the first Saturday of February every year. I have missed the race by less than a week, but the conditions are outstanding, even if my conditioning is not up to the level they exhibit—we had limited snow cover in Maine, and I, little time on skis. I thoroughly enjoyed the tour around the lake and have kept the race on my list of future endeavors. Maris, Ilmars, and especially young Matīss are extremely patient with me as I fall off the pace through the last hills with a couple kilometers to the finish and I rejoice as we return to the start area. The workout has the effect of tiring me, which seems to help with my adjustment to the 7 hours' time difference from home.

I visit the 12th klase we had been corresponding with and the session goes so well, I find myself talking with the 9th klase as well, and later trading songs with the 11th klase which includes Maris's daughter Elina, who also serves as a translator at home when Maris's English fails him. After singing and playing the guitar with the latter class, three of the girls insist on a song of their own with two singing perfect harmony and the third accompanying on the piano. Such talent!

Jānis Polis, a historian who is an expert on regional history and has written extensively on the Rātminders family stops at school and we discuss (through translation by my English teaching friends) some of what I know about my ancestry, and how little it is. Polis seems somewhat reserved and reticent to share his work, including the text "Pie tēvu zemes dārgās" (the title taken from a song by local composer Emīls Dārziņš), and after he leaves, I'm advised that he fears I will somehow steal his work for a publication of his own. This of course, turns out to be true as I mention it here, although it was not my goal at the time, and I've given him credit in any case.

Mirdza takes me to the home of Inguna Bauere, a writer who is working on a biography of Andžs Rātminders' daughter Līze. Her extensive writing focuses on the women behind the famous men of Latvian literati. Inguna agrees to send me a digital version of "Skolas Līze," and later it reveals an interesting facet of the Rathminder family which I will cover later.

The second afternoon, the headmaster invites me for coffee and pastry in her office. Velga, my English teaching counterpart, translates, as the headmaster does not speak English. Marija is roughly my age and has been in her position for over 30 years. She is warm, yet officious, commanding attention and respect. She presents me with three gifts, all produced locally: a history of Vecpiebalga written by the local writer I had already met, a unique wood sculpture resembling a sort of totem and created by a local artist and a mug with the community's name and symbol—the spinning wheel, a product the town was once known for—produced by a local ceramic manufacturer.

Our discussion is polite and centers a little on Andžs Rātminders, but more on recounting my whirlwind 2-day visit. Marija, in spite of her tenure with the school is obviously in awe of my ancestor's legacy.

As we talk, I cannot help but reflect on my childhood in the 1950s, my adolescence in the 60s, and my young adulthood in the 70s and 80s, when the threat of US-Soviet conflict was dominant and ever-present in the news. The image of Nikita Khrushchev banging his shoe on the rostrum at the United Nations in New York flashes through my head, as does the picture of John and Bobby Kennedy agonizing over the Cuban Missile Crisis. I also remember the bluster of President Reagan's line in Berlin: "Mr. Gorbachev, tear down this wall," knowing full well that the words of a Maine schoolgirl named Samantha Smith, in a letter to Yuri Andropov, were possibly more powerful to people in this part of the world.

As our conversation winds down, I marvel at my being here. I mention that as an elementary school student, we knew very little about Soviet Europe and I would never have imagined visiting here; that the USSR was considered our enemy, and we had air raid drills where we hid under our desks to prepare for the bombing that seemed so imminent. Velga translated and Marija smiled and replied very simply: "As a girl, we did the same." Twenty years after the fall of the Berlin Wall, I knew in this very moment that the great specter of my childhood, the Iron Curtain, had been lifted.

Within a couple months another curtain would dissolve on my return home, as I was surveying a relatively new online resource consisting of the digitized records of all 19th century Latvian churches. In the 1850 German records of the St. John's Church in Riga, in the section for baptisms for the month of September, listing #344, I find the christening of Augusta Dorothea, daughter of Johann Rathminder and his wife Marie Louise nee Jacobsohn, and the identity of my great grandmother's heritage is revealed.

Chapter Thirteen
Andžs Rātminders
(1805-1887)

Vecpiebalga's Friendly Schoolteacher

Andžs Rātminders

Andžs Rātminders' ascendency to the position of teacher and sexton of the Vecpiebalga parish school owes in equal parts to his talents and the modest development of education in the Livonian region of the Russian Empire. Certainly, this son of Andžs and Marija (Marie) Rātminders of the Zeikari farmstead had potential beyond his years, and the progressive pastor of the parish, Johann Friedrich Schilling, recognized and nurtured the talents of his young protégé. Andžs was one of the brightest minds in the neighborhood and when a position opened in the school, Pastor Schilling was quick to tap him for the position.

The school itself was a meager remnant of Swedish rule of the late 17th and early 18th century. The Swedish presence, which ended with the transfer of the Baltic territories to Peter the Great as a final settlement of the Northern War in 1721, was marked by an effort to formalize the relationship between German manor owners and their Latvian workers. One aspect of this initiative was the requirement to educate all workers, although males were the primary beneficiaries. Education fell naturally to the leaders of the Church, specifically the German Lutheran pastors. After the territory became part of the Russian Empire, the tsar encouraged the continuation of this practice as well as the domination of the Baltic German landowners and Lutheran pastors.

By the time Andžs Rātminders became a teacher in 1823 at the age of 18, the school was a portion (interesting that the Google translation of the Latvian words suggests it was a "scourge") of the basement of the local Inn with very little space or separation from the pub that existed there at the time. The students would study, eat and sleep in the school quarters, and had little space for any activity or the dirty bags of straw on which they slept. Within a few years the Inn could no longer be used and the school was housed in the parsonage until 1832 when a new building was erected on land reserved by previous Swedish edict for the church sexton.

True to his potential, Andžs not only devoted his energy to the education of his students but the beautification of the school property. He stressed language, geography, history and culture, as well as religion and music. In the latter discipline he taught polyphonic singing and established a youth choir to compliment his organ playing in church. And his horticultural work transformed the school plot from forest and undergrowth to land as thick and lovely as an English Garden.

Of the 8 children of Andžs and Marija of the Zeikari farmstead, Andžs (1805-1887) was apparently the first to reach adulthood. Jānis (1797) and Made (1802) preceded him but died young as did Marija later (1810). Andžs was followed by younger brothers Jēkabs (1808), Jānis (1812) and Matīss (1819) as well as younger sister Anna (1815). In all likelihood, Andžs was his brothers' teacher and certainly Jānis benefitted from his brother's tutelage, moving to Riga and becoming a teacher himself. While Andžs moved to the village on the school property, Jēkabs and Matīss worked the family farm well beyond the death of their parents in the 1840s.

The peasants in Livland were generally known by their given name and the farmstead they came from, so that Andžs' father was Andžs of Zeikari. Under the reign of Tsar Alexander I, land reforms were instituted to formalize the relationship between German manor owners and the peasants who worked for them. Although war with Napoleon delayed full implementation, the reforms effectively abolished serfdom in Livland by 1819. Over the next decade, contractual relationships between landowners and peasants required that the latter adopt surnames.

This 'naming' took place by 1829 and for Andžs, apparently "Rātminders" was chosen as a surname. I find no reference of the surname prior to this date. Unfortunately, translation of the name, in either the official low German of the day or Latvian, has eluded the reason for this choice. It is apparently a compound word and three possibilities have been offered. One implies a low-level official of the town council (from the Latvian 'rātē:' a lesser official), a second translates more loosely to advice or counsel (from the German 'rat') and a third suggests not very thrifty and implies installments, perhaps reflecting the patriarch's financial status with the landowner. Another possibility derives from the prolific production of spinning wheels in the Piebalga region.

In addition to teaching, gardening and work in the church, Andžs also found time to gather news of the day and publish it in newspapers. His journalistic work led to friendships with Ansis Leitans and others who would spearhead the advent of Latvian language newspapers and literature. He quickly became well-respected for his work and his opinions. This regard manifested itself in 1837 when St. John's parish school hired Jānis Rātminders primarily on the reputation of his older brother.

Literacy, culture, faith and music were the cornerstones of Andžs work. By the end of the 1830s, illiteracy was mostly eradicated in Vecpiebalga and Andžs gave the Latvian language, thought to be crude and vulgar by Baltic Germans, equal standing to the official German of the day. German continued to be the language of the educated and cultured but Latvian was developed in written and literary forms in Latvia through the mid-19th century and it was the determination of Andžs Rātminders and others that laid the groundwork for the development of the language. According to the 1897 census, 92% of Latvians were literate, one of the highest literacy rates in the Russian Empire.

After a decade of teaching, Andžs turned his attention to starting a family and married Ede Korneta, 8 years his junior. As with his parents, 8 children were born of the marriage and 5 daughters reached adulthood: Marija (born 1833), Anna (1838), Maija or Maja (1841), Līze (1848) and Karline (1850). Daughter Ede (1835) died at age 10, and sons Jānis (1843) and Andžs (1845) younger still.

Although the children were spread over a period of 17 years, the family put a strain on the small quarters provided in the school for its teacher. For this reason, Ede Rātminders was looking for substantial suitors for her daughters, so that they would not have to struggle with poverty while raising their own families. While Marija's husband Peteris Gailitis was a successful farmer, successive suitors met with increasing expectations. Anna married Dr. Andžs Jānis Jurjāns, and Maija was betrothed to Kārlis Sancbergs, a merchant. Karline, youngest, married a protégé of her father, Andžs Antons Tuluijs, a teacher and poet.

Līze, second youngest and most attractive, presented the greatest challenge for her parents. Intelligent, with a beautiful singing voice and acting ability, and an outgoing personality, Līze is regarded to have had 42 suitors! One, Andrejs Pumpers, who served as a land surveyor for a number of years in Vecpiebalga, went on to publish "Lāčplēsis" or "The Bearslayer," the iconic epic poem of a free Latvia. Others dedicated literary or musical compositions to her. Līze maintained the most interest in Matīss Kaudzitis, the 11th child of a poor peasant, who her parents could not approve of even after he became a successful teacher and writer. Only after Matīss and his brother, Reinis Kaudzitis, published the first Latvian novel, the successful "Mērnieku Laiki" ("Time of the Land Surveyors")—and after Andžs' death—did Ede relent and Līze and Matīss were married at age 46 in 1896!

As Andžs' family grew, so did his influence in Latvian education and culture, in spite of his never leaving the rural village of Vecpiebalga. His students became regarded as educators, writers, poets, musicians and composers, politicians, military leaders and sea captains, and went on to influence another generation of notable citizens. The National movement, which began in the mid-19th century and was influenced by many who studied with or knew Andžs Rātminders, culminated with the first period of Latvian independence from 1920-1940.

Chapter Fourteen

Riga/Hamburg - Summer 2010

Returning to Latvia in the summer of 2010 seemed almost a necessity to me in an effort to keep the momentum of my research going. Discovering Augusta's birth record in St. John's Church in Riga propelled me to look in new and diverse directions and inspired more depth in my efforts. The only questions were when I would return and for how long. A month in the middle of the summer were the answers and I worked to great distraction on planning my great research trip.

Beth would be staying home to work while I visited museums and archives to piece together more of the Maddaus/Rathminder family history. I also was determined to trace Johann Karl Ludwig Maddaus back to his origins in Hamburg, Germany and employed the research our Canadian relative Eileen Marcil had provided towards that end.

To some extent the results were startling, a real revelation in terms of the breadth and depth of information I gained in the process, but the experience was akin to going down the rabbit hole and not re-emerging. And this writing is just part of the 'wonderland' I've been exposed to. Armed with the identity of Augusta Dorothea Rathminder Maddaus' parents and the knowledge of her father's ethnic background, I had a totally new perspective on our Baltic heritage and the loss of crucial parts of ethnic makeup. Questions upon questions continue to arise.

German church records call him Jahn Rathminder or Johan Rathminder, but in Latvian, his name is Jānis Rātminders and I'll use the Latvian from this point forward.

The national library archives provided a wealth of information on our great, great grandfather in part due to the number of publications he had a hand in and part due to the documentation from a previous researcher. A library bibliographer patiently led me through each and every item, explaining the significance of each. The detail is provided in a section later in this manuscript.

To find that our ancestor was a prolific writer, poet, translator, and teacher was only part of the story, for he was also identified as one who was not only educated and fluent in German, the academic language of the times, but he also was determined to elevate the Latvian language, the language of the peasants, to the same level.

His published works, printed mostly in the old black-type, and written in the indigenous Latvian language represent ground-breaking work at a time when German dominated academia and mercantile society and Russian was the language of the Empire. Indeed, the terms Latvia and Latvian were not widely used. Jānis took part in the First Awakening when peasants from the indigenous tribes of the various regions of what is now called Latvia, began to identify as a unified people with a (somewhat) common language and culture. His contribution was in literature and literacy.

How this crucial family history failed to make its way to America and, especially, failed to be known by our 2nd generation of Americans was the result of a number of factors, but seeing the published works of Jānis Rātminders all gathered in front of me obliterated the time and distance they might have traveled. It is not just knowing the part he played in his world, it is also having tangible evidence of his life and times that he as an individual touched and shaped. No matter what level of knowledge is passed from generation to generation, having the actual writings and artifacts spread out in front of you is an awe-inspiring experience.

Tilting back to the Maddaus side of our ancestry, I scanned the airBaltic pricing for an economical round-trip ticket to Hamburg for a three-day, two-night stay in the city of Johann Karl Ludwig's birth and with Eileen Marcil's information, made a list of sites to visit.

I booked a hotel across from the central rail station, as I could then conveniently use the train from the airport to downtown. The hotel was on the edge of the St. George district, which I would later find was the area many of the 9/11 terrorists had been radicalized. Nine years after the attack on America the area was still populated by immigrants from the Middle East.

My primary goal was to see St. Michealis Kirche (St. Michael's Church) the iconic cathedral overlooking the Elbe, west of the city center. This is church where Johann Karl Ludwig Maddaus was baptized in 1820 and likewise his father Georg Maddaus in 1798.

Eileen's research with the help of the archives of Hamburg, identified the church, as well as two street addresses for Georg and Henriette and one for his parents. My expectations were again somewhat limited. Hamburg, like Liepzig and Dresden and other German cities was firebombed by American and British Air Force to hasten the end of World War Two and I had read accounts of the horrific scenes—people being vaporized as they walked the streets and centuries-old landmarks destroyed indiscriminately—and had a limited concept of what 2010 in Hamburg might consist of.

I used Kurt Vonnegut's novel "Slaughterhouse-Five" as a standard offering in my senior English classes. Vonnegut's unique disjointed narrative written in an attempt to tell the horrors of experiencing the destruction of Dresden has always been haunting to me. Combined with the story of my New Hampshire friend Otto Ninow, whose mother committed suicide not long after the bombing, this had the effect of melding with our family line that 'all records of our family had been lost in the war.' Vonnegut's description of dead bodies in a flaming funeral pyre and the innocent alter-ego Billy Pilgrim determined to 'concentrate on the happy moments of his life' juxtaposed in terrible irony. Otto learning that the fact that all radio broadcasting ceased after the bombing was a sign to his mother that her son was dead and life no longer had meaning. Both estimated the death toll at well over 100,000 as the city was jam-full of refugees fleeing the Soviet army to the east.

For me, walking the streets of Hamburg—a beautiful 21st century German city—included aspects of great enjoyment, stunning revelations and a sense of doom.

My discoveries grounded me in our Hamburg family history.

The baptismal font in St. Michael's Church dates to the mid-18th century. And though the church had suffered damage in various wars over the centuries, it stands as a lasting monument to the city's history. This was the baptismal font where my great-great grandfather was christened, along his brother and sister, and their father, as well.

St. Michaelis Kirche baptismal font

I walked past the waterfront address for Georg and Henriette, now a two- level street lined with modern architecture and could only imagine the early 19th century waterfront. Then I walked up the hill past St. Michaels to the Backbrietergang neighborhood where two story houses dated to the 18th century era when Georg's family lived in the district.

St. Michael's baptismal font and Backbrietergang strasse. Two palpable connections to a heritage once lost through emigrations and wars.

Near Hamburg City Hall, a "Stuttgartar Weindorf Festival" full of booths for food and merchandise from southern Germany was my last stop and I enjoyed some bratwurst, spätzle and cider and listened to musicians playing folk music in their lederhosen under a tent full of festival goers. I thought of how great it was to see the city of our origin and enjoy one of the happy moments in my life.

On return from my three-day sojourn to Hamburg, I pivoted back to research on the Rātminders side of the family and especially the Latvian Archives and Library. This has been a regular occurrence. Each time I delve deep into the life of Johann Maddaus another twist takes me to the Rātminders family, before going back to the Maddaus ancestry again.

Archival work seems like going to the doctor or dentist. Lots of waiting, testing and at times, uncertain results. The National Archives and State Archives provided some details into the vital statistics associated with Marija Rātminders and her residence on Slokas iela. The information, even her passport after all the waiting, was interesting though not earth-shattering. This documented the life of my great grandmother's sisters, post-independence, which we were at least familiar with through my grandparents visit in 1912 with my 3-year old father in tow, and Uncle Oscar's visit after the war. The data supported what little family knowledge we had.

The Library Archives, located then on Jēkabs iela adjacent to parliament, opened a whole new aspect of the Rātminders heritage that was totally unknown to us. Here a research specialist named Renate, patiently led me through a series of documents directly relating to Jānis Rātminders. She had a numbered list that had been reviewed by at least one other inquirer—perhaps Jānis Polis or another historian--and she gave me ample time with each exhibit and answered my questions as they arose. It was a treasure-trove of writings by our ancestor.

Foremost among the items were a number of original copies of the narrative poetry entitled "Story Songs" ("Stāstu dziesmas"), published in 1850. I'll discuss the work later in a later chapter, but will mention here that this was presented to me as one of the earliest of Latvian language literature published in the Russian Empire. Along with other examples of his work, it became apparent to me that what Johann Maddaus was to Baltic German Art, Jānis Rātminders was to early Latvian literature. And the discovery of these works broadened my understanding and connection to 19th Century Latvia.

This month of study, research and discovery could not have had a more profound impact on my understanding of our ancestry. In the years since, I have taken every opportunity to deepen my knowledge of these two ancestors and the times in which they lived.

But for all the new knowledge I gained in the streets and churches and archives and museums of Latvia, I had one more revelation coming to me. That would could from a promise made by Mirdza, my retired English teaching friend from Vecpiebalga, during my visit that winter. As I left her, Mirdza made a point to say "I may know a relative of yours, from the family of Rātminders."

Towards the end of my summer month in Latvia, I received an email from Mirdza confirming that a friend—a roommate, no less—from her university days was, indeed, a descendant of Jēkabs Rātminders, the brother of Andžs and Jānis, and further, that her friend's daughter would meet me in Riga.

Soon arrangements were made for me to meet with Lelde and for her to take me to Ikšķile to meet her mother Anda, Mirdza's dear friend. And so, totally by chance, I was introduced to the extended family of Augusta Rathminder Maddaus' Latvian relatives and a whole new world of discovery opened to me. And as anyone who has experienced knowing relatives from the old country knows, there is nothing quite like seeing it through their experiences.

Once again, thanks to Mirdza's promise, the story has new chapters and new colorful images to add to the tapestry that is our family history. But first, a biographical sketch of Jānis Rātminders.

Chapter Fifteen

Jānis Rātminders
(December 8, 1812 - October 8, 1880)
Teacher, Poet, Translator

Jānis Rātminders

For Jānis Rātminders, there was no greater joy than sharing his faith in God and love of learning with his fellow Latvians and his poetry exuded both of those qualities. But he was the product of three worlds and his daughter Augusta—our great grandmother—would depart for yet another when she left her family for a new life in America.

Jānis was brought up on the Zeikari farmstead just north of the village of Vecpiebalga, some 130 kilometers east of Riga. The farmstead sits on the windward side of a knoll that is the height of land to the west of Alauksts Lake. A short walk on the driveway down to the main road (P30) from Vecpiebalga to Cesis to the north, affords a panoramic view of the lake with the iconic white birch rimming its shore. To the west, the rivulet which becomes the Gauja River—the longest entirely in Latvia—winds through the fields from its source in Kaive, then north and east and again north and finally west on its meandering route to the Baltic Sea.

The 19th century Latvian landscape Jānis Rātminders was born into was not yet Latvia, but a part of the Russian Empire since the end of the Northern War which relinquished Swedish control of the eastern Baltic littoral in the 1720s. And yet the countryside was populated by Latvians and Germans. As the Latvian novelist Matīss Kaudzītes once noted, in these days the terms Latvian and German were equivalent to peasant and landowner, as the dominance of the latter established centuries before continued through the 19th century. At times the German presence was oppressive, but the influence of Swedish kings and Moravian brethren, along with the German Lutheran church, resulted in an increase in the literacy rate among Latvians. Literacy and refined culture were the domains of Germans and most education was conducted in German.

Jānis Rātminders (Johann or Jahn Rathminder in the German-language church records) was the third of four sons of Andžs and Marie Rathminder to reach adulthood—one sister did as well—and the second so named after an older sibling who died in infancy along. Jānis and Andžs were popular names in the Vidzeme countryside—Jānis' paternal grandfather was also Jānis and his oldest brother was Andžs. Though he was influenced by all his family, it was his brother Andžs who has the most lasting and profound impact on his life. Andžs, 7 years older than Jānis, was intelligent and multi-talented and when a teaching position became available at the local parish school, Andžs was chosen at the age of 18. He would become a legend in Latvian education as he continued in the role for 63 years, one the longest and far-reaching in history. So it would be Andžs who would teach his younger brother Jānis and mentor him in his own teaching career for years to come.

After completing his training under his brother's tutelage, Jānis sought further experience in Riga, the commercial and cultural center of the eastern Baltic region. Before long he secured a position teaching in the manor of Sasumuižā (Zasulauks) on the Pardaugava area of Riga across the Daugava River from the city center. By 1837 he secured a position at the St. John's parish in the old city, and he would continue there until the year of his death—over 42 years. Longevity was but one of his accomplishments as he took a prominent role in the literary movement in the Latvian language and what became known as the 'National Awakening,' which brought Latvian language, culture and literature into firm footing alongside German and Russian influences. To say Jānis was a member of the Latvian intelligentsia of the mid-19th century would be accurate, but fall short of describing his overall contribution to the national movement.

His literary connections most certainly were enhanced by his association with Pastor Hermans Treijs, the St. John's parish leader, who himself was a prolific writer. Treijs had began in 1832 to publish a weekly newspaper "Tas Latviesu Lauzu Draugs" ("Friend of the Latvian People") and continued its publication to at least 1846. Once Jānis began work in the parish school, he also became a regular contributor to the publication with stories and poetry written under his own byline and with pseudonyms of JR and 49. Examples of his work dating back to 1840 are on file in the National Library of Latvia, including "Good work, bad salary" and "Christmas message to students" in 1842, collaborations with Ansis Leitans on "Songs for Ludwig Schulz" and Pastor Hermans Treijs "Christmas Greetings" in 1844 and "Poems for Karl Hieronymus Schirren" in 1847. This collaboration would represent the beginning of a life-long friendship with Leitans which would further his writing career.

A collection of his pieces written for "Tas Latviesu Lauzu Draugs," including "Pretzels from Father" and "Grandfather's Life," became the basis for his publication in 1850 of "Stāstu dziesmas" ("Story Songs"), a book of poetic stories centered on a young Latvian lad named Juris. The stories take the form of parables which emphasize the virtues of hard work, education and faith, leading to an honorable life. While some historians mark the date of the first Latvian-language publication of poetry by a Latvian as that of Juris Alunans' "Dziesminas" (Poetry) in 1856, Jānis was clearly 6 years ahead of Alunans. Between 1850 and 1870 the percentage of such publications in the region went from single digits to 50 percent as the new generation of educated Latvians followed the lead of Rātminders and Alunans. A biography of Jānis Rātminders after his death by J. R. Kalniuks suggests that "Stāstu dziesmas" was widely read and admired, though it has been largely forgotten today.

The publication of Alunans' work and the establishment of the Latvian language newspaper "Mājas Viesis" (The House-Guest) by Jānis Rātminders' good friend and collaborator Ansis Leitans in 1856 marked the beginning of the first Latvian National Awakening which extended into the 1880s. Jānis was a significant contributor to Mājas Viesis, along with fellow teachers Juris Caunitis, Mikelis Ciritis and Jānis Katkins. Mājas Viesis was authorized by the new Tsar of Russia, Alexander II and became the first Latvian newspaper founded by Latvians and edited by Latvians. It evoked a sense of pride and excitement in the Latvian identity.

Soon after the founding of "Mājas Viesis," a succeeding generation of 'New Latvians' came on the scene, having all been educated at Dorpat (Tartu) University and given the opportunity to publish their writings in the new weekly paper. Now legendary figures such as KrisJānis Valdemars, Juris Alunans, KrisJānis Barons and Atis Kronvalds met regularly to discuss political, cultural and literary issues that were of interest to ethnic Latvians. This group was a reflection of an earlier regular gathering of intelligentsia including Jānis Rātminders, Ansis Leitans and others, often at Jānis' home, in the late 1830s and into the 1840s. While this early group met often, its progress was blunted by Tsar Nicholas II who felt threatened by a number of national movements in the Empire and directed local representatives to limit its meetings. Over the long term these intrepid Latvians influenced the next wave of the national movement.

The name Latvia (Latvija) became commonly used by 1862 and in the late 1860s the seeds of a new organization which became known as the Riga Latvian Association were sown. Jānis, though not as active in his younger days, was involved in the formation of this organization and wrote a song, "Kas mūsu spēks, / Kas mūsu pūles" ("In our power, in our efforts"), with music by Juliujs Purats, which was dedicated to the Association at its founding in 1868. By 1873, with the first National Song and Dance Festival, the Association was a well-established body in support of Latvian Nationalism.

In September 1846, Jānis married Maria Louise Jacobsohn, daughter of Adam and Maria Magdalena Jacobsohn who were long-time members of the St. John's parish. Jānis and Maria had 10 children over a period of 16 years. Our great, grandmother Augusta Dorothea Rathminder was the third and was named for a descendent of Gotthard Friedrich Stender, an 18th century Latvian grammarian and lexicographer. Although Jānis was active among Latvian language intellectuals, he also shared the trait of many of those in that he was immersed in German language and culture of the day as well. Augusta was more influenced by the German side of the house, as evidenced by her love of German romance novels, chiefly among them "Ingo" by Gustav Freytag, the source of our grandfather's given name as well as that of his sister Freida. To his death my father always referred to her as his 'German' grandmother.

Jānis kept in close contact with his brother Andžs until his death in 1880. An interesting anecdote surrounding their relationship revolved around the hiring of the great Latvian nationalist orator Atis Kronvalds as a teacher in Vecpiebalga. Andžs knew of Kronvalds stature in the national movement, but wanted to be assured that this great young voice of Latvia was a well-rounded individual, versed in history, philosophy, the arts and religion, so he consulted with his best resource in Riga, his brother Jānis. On Jānis' recommendation Kronvalds was hired and served in the Vecpiebalga parish school until his death at the relatively young age of 37 in 1875.

Jānis retired to new home on Slokas iela (Woodcock Street) in Agenkalns area, not far from Zasulauks manor where he first worked on his arrival in Riga. He is buried in the Martina Cemetery across the street from his home.

Chapter Sixteen

Līgo and Jāņi Midsummer Holidays - 2011
Early Lessons in What It Means to be Latvian

No doubt, I was making the transition from identifying with the German, English, Scotch-Irish heritage tags I grew up with, to understanding the meaning behind those labels and with the addition of Latvian ancestors to our family tree where only uncertain placeholders had resided. The knowledge of the lives of Jānis Rātminders and his brother Andžs, their parents Andžs and Marija and the Zeikari farmstead overlooking the shores of Alauksts Lake, had become palpable, living evidence of our family heritage and I was becoming fully engaged with learning the cultural intricacies of both our Baltic German and Latvian ancestors through the lens of 21st Century Latvian culture.

If you have a relative in a distant unfamiliar state or foreign land, you can have no better than Lelde, and on our subsequent visits to Latvia she has been a welcoming presence and enthusiastic teacher of all things Latvian. And that is not to say other of our relatives have not been as welcoming, but she just takes such great care to help us understand the country she is so proud of.

Perhaps it is her vocation as a historian for the Occupation Museum but even more likely it is because she is simply such a nice person. Part of it is her personality, serious and studious, cheerful and friendly, all wrapped up in one package. And Gatis, her husband, is equally welcoming if more reserved and cautious with his English. Lelde's mother, aunt and uncle, and other relatives I have met from their age group do not generally know English and so she and Gatis are especially valuable to us during our visits.

Lelde and Gatis are of a generation that has adopted the English as a working language along with their native Latvian and Latvia's unofficial second language, Russian. With the advent of Latvia's entry into NATO and the European Union, with English as its common language, and the re-independence of Latvia a few years earlier, the country looked westward and made English readily available in the schools and for those in business and politics. Those from my generation--now in their 60s and older--were not likely to have studied English and I am often asked if I know German, as that was the most likely third language. Of course, it is common to know three or more languages here, as in much of Europe. I fumble along with one, my high school French of little consequence.

Lelde works professionally as a digital archivist for the Museum of the Occupation of Latvia in Riga, eliciting and recording testimonies of the broad swath of Latvians who were displaced during World War Two and the period of Soviet rule from the end of the War to 1991 or so. The stories are varied and breathtaking from treacherous crossings of the Baltic Sea to Sweden during the War, escapes to displaced persons (DP) camps in Germany at the end of the War, settlement in Western countries such as Canada, Australia, the UK and US, and deportation (often without returning) to Siberia during one of Stalin's purges. Lelde has the talent and insight to record these testimonies and produce, along with her colleagues, a number of videos providing a sampling of the catalog.

I have more to relate about this fascinating work later in this book, but here I want to take a different tact, because it is thanks to Lelde and Gatis that I have grown to appreciate Latvia's love affair with the land--the hills and fields and forests, the rivers and lakes and peat bogs, and the sea that borders it on two sides. While a large majority of Latvians live in Riga, the capital, virtually all, whether city dwellers or not, love the countryside, the hills, and the sea. They might be Rigans in residence, but they identify with the country village they or their parents came from.

The year after my double solo visits in 2010, Beth and I returned in 2011 to do some more exploring and to introduce her to my new-found relatives. One of the first days after our arrival we attended a birthday party for Lelde in their hometown of Ikšķile. The setting was a family plot of land near the Daugava River not far from the village, where her mother and father had built a small summer cottage to facilitate picnics. Nearby, on the banks of the Daugava, you can see the location of St. Meinhard's church in the middle of the river, the first settlement of Christians in Latvia dating to the 12th century.

Whether the usual birthday gathering or not, most all of Lelde's family attended, her mother, uncle, sister and her husband and young son, along with other relatives from another distinct branch of the Rātminders family. All are descendants of Jēkabs Rātminders, a brother of Jānis and Andžs. From one relative we now knew 20 or so, and the number would only grow. And a year before, we knew of none of them.

Ikskile Birthday Party

The party featured a beautiful spread of food as picnics often do, much conversation which Lelde would translate for us, and a walk along the river. As the afternoon went on the clouds came in and eventually greeted us with a hailstorm with nuggets a quarter inch in diameter, the entire group of us huddled under a tarp-like covering until the sun re-appeared almost as quickly as it departed.

As we were planning to head back to the train and our hotel in Riga, Lelde asked if we had plans for Līgo a few days later. I had learned this was the name for the Latvian celebration of the summer solstice, which is a two-day national holiday in the country. She invited us to attend a gathering hosted by one of her colleagues (subject to his approval) in Liepupe north of Riga toward the Estonian border. Before we knew it, we were on the road to Liepupe and the event of a lifetime.

Perhaps due to the topography and geography of the country, Latvians over the centuries have been over-run by numerous invaders--Norse, Rusk, Poles, Lithuanians, Swedes, Russians, Germans to name just a few--and seem to have been able to blend with the most recent occupiers. This is my impression, rather than an established fact, but it certainly applies to their celebration of the Summer Solstice, a pagan event which has modern ties to St. John's Day on the Christian Calendar. Since the final Crusade which overtook the Baltics in the 12th and 13th centuries, the Christian celebration of the birth of John the Baptist has provided cover for the Latvian celebration of Līgo (Midsummer's Night) and Jāņi diena (Midsummer's Day). Līgo references the night before the St. John's holiday and that is when all the fun takes place. St. John's Day for Latvians is more of an extension of the celebration with the latter part of the day to provide some recovery.

We met Lelde and Gatis in route and stopped at a grocery store for food, thinking we were supplying our own needs, but later finding it would be added to a giant communal buffet. Liepupe is east and north of Riga and the drive took us past Saulkrasti and its beach where we have stopped before and on the route to Estonia, so we were getting more and more acclimated to the highways and byways of Latvia.

Arrival at the site in Liepupe was set for late afternoon as Lelde and Gatis were to help prepare for the evening's activities and we along with them. The celebration takes place on the high point of the farmstead, although no buildings remained from earlier times. Lelde explained that Līgo extends through to sunrise the next morning and that we were not obligated to stay though encouraged to do so. Festivities get started closer to sunset and extend to sunrise the next day. It is often said that everyone in Riga heads to the country for the night's celebration and while that is not totally true--Riga has its own boisterous gathering along the Daugava in the Old City and another across the river in a park in Agenkalns--we certainly saw a population animated for the event, both in the city and the country..

Preparations involved a variety of tasks and a number of folks were involved in preparing the fire circle, painting the unique designs on the rocks, setting up a fire for the caraway seed cheese preparation, and filling the banquet table.

Beth went with Lelde to gather windflowers which were then woven into headpieces for the women to wear, while I helped Gatis around the fire ring. Our job was to sharpen the bases of a large supply of freshly cut, 2-3-meter-long, white birch saplings to then install in two concentric rings around the firepit, the purpose of which was a mystery to me as we were doing it. We probably worked for an hour or more on this task and it took a while to take shape but as we neared completion the area was transformed into a sort of labyrinth around the outside of a second concentric ring of stones, 2 meters or so from the stone fire ring itself. Our rings of white birch saplings had openings at either end to allow movement to the center.

We took breaks to survey the other preparations and Lelde patiently explained the significance of each, to the best of her ability, while at the same time conversing with all she met, her ability to seamlessly go from Latvian to English ever apparent. We saw an alternate fire being prepared in a basket mounted on the end of an 8-9-meter pole, to be suspended in the air and lit at sunset, while our host and hostess also prepared the firewood structure in the fire pit, surrounded by a wreath of oak branches, ferns and purple lupine flowers. Each rock was painted with a unique symbol and greens we shredded and scattered around the very outside of the ring to ward off spirits.

Beth and Lelde at Liepupe

Gatis and I rejoined Lelde and Beth and we admired each other's work, especially their headpieces made of yellow and purple wildflowers, grasses and herbs. It was then time to prepare for the opening ceremony, Lelde and Gatis changing into traditional dress and the gathering of everyone adjacent to the fire ring.

The ceremony that followed began with a circular dance of sorts done to the music of a fiddler, as the group wound its way ever closer to the entrance to the first birch ring opening. Ultimately, we found our way through the two birch rings and to the ring between the two stone rings. At that point we stopped and Jānis and Inese, our hosts, began the ceremony with a number of proclamations (in Latvian, of course) leading to the lighting of the fire. Jānis has the perfect name for this and as with all men with the given name Jānis, wore the symbolic oak wreath, distinguishing him doubly in his duties.

Our collective purpose on this shortest night of the year was to shepherd the light from sunset to sunrise. A symbolic flame is passed among all those gathered and Jānis proclaims the value of the light and the coming of the dawn in sacred terms. Once the bonfire is lit, we join in a variety of ancient folk songs all dedicated to Līgo. It is a liturgy borne of tradition and nature. Taking part envelops you in the warmth and depth of the community and its most sacred connections.

The Flame

It is a night of miracles at the height of nature's power, with a unique charm and promise for the future.

The beliefs surrounding Midsummer Night are ancient and varied. Some of the many are characterized in the following from one Latvian travel website:

- On Summer Solstice Eve, unmarried women are expected to weave two crowns of flowers, go to the river at midnight, and toss the crowns into the water. If they come together, she will soon be married, if not, then she will not soon be married.

- On Summer Solstice Eve, unmarried people must throw a crown of oak branches into an apple tree. The number of times that the crown falls to the ground represents the number of years before the person will get married.

- It is said that at midnight on Summer Solstice Eve, livestock talks about the fate of people.

- If you want your hair to grow long, then you must pour a few mugs of beer on your hair at midnight on Summer Solstice Eve.

- Grass grows better where celebrants have crossed meadows on Summer Solstice Eve.

- On the morning of Summer Solstice Day, cut the stem of a fern at the very foundation. You will see a letter on the cut part of the stem, and that will be the first letter of the name of your future husband or wife.
- When beer is brewed for Summer Solstice purposes, strangers must not be allowed to be present for the process, because then the beer will not brew properly.
- The owner of the farm must be the first to approach the keg of beer. If someone else does so, then he will be persecuted by problems.
- On Summer Solstice Eve, people go to pastures to sing songs and eat cheese to bless the livestock.
- On the morning of Summer Solstice day, girls wash their faces in the dew of wheat plants so that their faces are clean and white.
- Dew on Summer Solstice Eve is very important. People who wash themselves in the dew become beautiful. If the dew falls into your shoes, it will turn into silver and gold.
- Ferns bloom with brilliant blossoms on Summer Solstice Eve. If you find one, you will be eternally happy, and all of your wishes will come true.
- If you find a fern with golden blossoms on Summer Solstice Eve, you can make one wish that will come true.
- If you want to know everything about the world, then find a fern that blooms at midnight, pick it, use a knife to cut your arm, and put the blossom into the wound, then letting it heal. Then you will forever know everything that is happening in the world.
- Around midnight on Summer Solstice Eve, wade through some water. There will be money in your shoes the next morning.
- On Summer Solstice Eve, mountain ash branches must be used to decorate fields so that envious people cannot do anything bad to them.

- Neighbor women must converse one Summer Solstice Eve, because then they will not quarrel during the entire next year.

https://www.celotajs.lv/en/c/wrth/traditions/events/midsummer/beliefs

I cannot confirm many (if any) of these but do not doubt them either. We were certainly treated to a magical experience.

Once the ceremony has been completed, the festive banquet table greets the assembled and we share in food and drink from the accumulated gifts of all the attendees. Caraway cheese made in the iron pots over open fires are a special treat, as are the dark rye breads and local beers, for those who choose to imbibe.

As we eat, visitors from nearby villages greet us with a new round of folk songs and join us for a time before continuing on their way. And a commotion is stirred by the raising of the elevated bonfire in an adjacent field.

I admit to feeling my age and/or still suffering from the 7 hours jetlag, and around midnight both Beth and I realized we would not last through until dawn, so we bid our hosts goodbye and drive back to our hotel in Riga, somewhat tired but also refreshed in the enchanting aura of the experience. In doing so we are vulnerable to one other belief: "Those who sleep on Midsummer night (Jāņi) are doomed to sleep the whole summer--in other words, be lazy." It is my hope that we received some sort of pass on this one!

Līgo is an event that is firmly fixed in our memories, and we would later come to appreciate the other lesser festivals of the Latvian calendar and celebrate each in a quiet way, so far from the land they originated from.

Latvian folk songs, known as "dainas," reflect the tradition of festivals and thanks to Krišjānis Barons (1835-1923) they were collected and catalogued for posterity's sake, over 200,000 in number. Many relate to the Midsummer festival. Here is one I especially love:

> Young lads, young girls,
> Don't sleep on Midsummer night,
> Then in the morning you'll see
> How the sun sparkles.
> LD 33209

As I said, it is magical.

Chapter Seventeen

Latvian Literature -
"And whoever writes will rejoice"

My first few trips to Vecpiebalga and subsequent 'discovery' of our great, great grandfather Jānis Rātminders opened the door to much of what is foundational in Latvian language literature. Rātminders' "Story Songs" and other poetry written for publication in the Latvian language newspaper "Majas Viesis" represents some of the earliest narrative poetry in the language and present significant slices of life in 19th century Latvia. They are also part and parcel of the early years of the First National Awakening, if you will, and Jānis was fully cognizant of this desire on the part of his countrymen to establish their own identity beyond their servitude to the German Landtag and as subjects of the Russian Tsar.

Jānis Rātminders' influence in Riga was to a great extent germinated in the Piebalgan countryside under the tutelage of his brother Andžs. Vecpiebalga and the surrounding farmsteads and hamlets is considered by some scholars to be the cradle of 19th Latvian culture. I discovered this early in my investigation of Andžs Rātminders and his daughter, Līze, and later with the knowledge of the great orator Atis Kronvalds and lyric poet Kārlis Skalbe.

Līze had a unique connection to two of the most significant writers of the period. One of her many suitors was Andrejs Pumpurs (1841-1902), author of "Bearslayer" ("Lāčplēsis," 1888), the iconic epic poem which is integral to Latvian national identity. After many years and a trail of suitors, she finally married another towering author of Latvian literature, Matīss Kaudzites (1848-1926), who, with his brother Reinis

(1839-1920) wrote "Time of the Land Surveyors" ("Mērnieku laiki," 1879), the first Latvian language novel, which documented in fictional form the pivotal period in the 19th century when peasants were given freedom from serfdom and ownership of land, in itself a new bondage of sorts.

In "Bearslayer," Pumpers uses Homeric canto form to tell the tale of a Latvian hero as he was "prophesied in ancient times," according to the gods who follow both his fate and the fate of the Latvia nation. Suckled as a baby at "a she-bear's milky breast," and raised to the age of 18 by the Lielvarde Lord, he saves his father as his first heroic deed, upon which he is sent to the Castle of Wisdom at Aizkraukle. Subsequent cantos outline his deeds and obstacles as he fights for the soul of the Latvian nation against its unwelcome occupiers--the German landowners. Bearslayer is last seen in mortal battle with the Black Knight as he throws the invader into the Daugava River, but then is dragged down with him.

> The waters made a cracking sound,
>
> The waves surged high and took the pair,
>
> And, in their fight together bound,
>
> Into the depths they vanished there!

The promise of Bearslayer's return buoyed the Latvian nation to its independence,

> When Strangers no more rule the folk,
>
> In Latvia Freedom's day will dawn;
>
> When Latvians no more bear the yoke,
>
> Their Golden Age will be reborn.

and helped it endure the long Soviet occupation. Indeed, it was the production of "Rokoperas Lāčplēsis" (1988) with libretto by Māra Zālīte and music by Zigmars Liepiņš, that propelled the music revolution and the Latvian Front to re-independence at the fall of the Soviet Union. Zālīte and Liepiņš were able to convince the Soviet powers that this struggle with German invaders was their struggle, although Latvians knew the struggle extended to the Soviets themselves, and continues to this day.

The translation of Lāčplēsis to the English Bearslayer by Arthur Cropley is an adept and faithful adaptation of the epic, making its tale accessible to Anglophiles. Cropley has no Latvian ancestry, but developed an abiding interest in Latvian culture and literature to the point that he studied the language and eventually published his version of Bearslayer. Critics would suggest it is not a direct translation, but for an appreciation of the epic it works well

"Mērnieku laiki," to my knowledge, has not been translated to English, and that's unfortunate. Maybe someday! I have been led to believe that the colloquial language contained in it would be extremely difficult to translate, perhaps like trying to translate Mark Twain's 'Huck Finn' into a foreign language. Certainly, it would be daunting to make those dialects accessible.

The history of rural 19th century Latvian lands is pretty unique in the fact that peasants (members of the ethnic Latvian tribes) were caught in the crosshairs of German land ownership and Russian rule. Either group was likely to impact the lives of Latvians of the day. It wasn't until 1819 that serfs in Kurzeme and Vidzeme were emancipated, and not until 1864 in Latgale. A registration requirement led to 'the naming' of ethnic Latvians in the 1820s, the first time many had surnames, rather than just an identification by their homestead.

Tsar Nicholas I was very suspect of any nationalization within the Empire but when his son Alexander II assumed the throne in 1855, liberalization of the nation gradually took hold, only to end with his assassination in 1881. Alexander III was intent on tightening control and introduced Russification early in his rule, resulting in Russian language requirements in public records and schools.

With this history as a backdrop, the surveying and transfer of farmlands to Latvians was of great interest to the Kaudzitis brothers.

Working for a period of years, Reinis and Matīss produced this first Latvian novel describing peasant and farmstead life of the middle of the century. In it they included a love story, centered on the character Liene and her parents--based on our great grandmother's cousin Līze and her parents Andžs and Ede Rathminder. The novel is said to combine a number of themes and the Brothers Kaudzitis describe the economic conditions, the power of money, cultural events, language boundaries combined with rich descriptions of everyday life.

Jānis Rātminders' earlier "Story Songs" ("Stasu dziemas," 1850) was less expansive, though perhaps no less ambitious. His goal was to describe slices of country life from the mid-19th century and in doing so, relate themes of faith and morality. As a school teacher, he addressed the text to his natural audience, children. And as a native of Vecpiebalga, he was determined to prove to the German dominated intelligentsia that the written Latvian language could be elevated to educational and literary use.

Examples of the vignettes in "Story Songs" illustrate his method. In "Pretzels from Father," young Juris is excited to have his father return home from the market, many miles away in Riga:

"Mum, Father's coming home".

Cries the boy Juris happily.

"Home from Riga!

Hurry, Gusts!

See there, our horse's legs moving!

Where's my fur coat?

Where's my cap, my stick?

Mum, where'd you put it?

Whoever knows

Should look for it:

I'm running off to meet Father!"

Father is both happy to see Juris and learn what has transpired while he was away from home, but concerned about his welfare as the boy meets him in the muddy and cold day:

> "Oh, son, have you come out
>
> In the mud, in the wet?
>
> Barefoot! Where are you running
>
> On such a cold day?
>
> Ah yes, you've come to meet Father,
>
> And you're crying already from joy.
>
> Come here then! Get in the cart
>
> And tell me how are things at home?
>
> Sit here up front
>
> And hold on when the horse starts running.
>
> Many a fellow caught unawares
>
> Has chanced to fall from a cart.
>
> How's your dear mother?
>
> Is she well? What's Grandpa doing?
>
> Is Klāvs home from his duties for the lord?
>
> Is Viļums already ploughing the field?
>
> Is Godfather hurrying to build the storehouse?
>
> See, they're waiting for us at home,
>
> All lined up by the door.

The whole family greets Father to learn of his travails and he comments on the care of the horse and its feeding

> And little Gusts, running about with joy;
>
> Like a swarm of bees, they've come together!
>
> Look, Krancis and Pakans come running, too,
>
> Barking loudly the one and the other.

> Good evening, dear wife! How've you been?
> See, I'm so wet and muddy!
> But are none of the lads home
> Who could unharness the horse?
> Call Grandpa, he'll manage
> To unload the things I've bought!
> Go, Mārtiņš, tie up the horse
> Where it can't reach the water
> And then groom its coat;
> After that you can feed him,
> Since water's bad for a horse,
> If it drinks while still hot from work.

Then Father presents the gifts chosen with great care for each member of the family:

> Grandpa's taken the chest inside;
> So, now you'll get presents from me.
> Come, my children, stand before me.
> Here's something for your tummies!
> Here, Jurka, a lollipop for you! And where's Gusts?
> Come here: a golden cross for you.
> Here's a couple of pies for Mada and Līze,
> And a pair of boots for Jurka, too;
> Here's thirty herring for Godmother,
> And Grandpa'll get some tobacco.
> Dear wife, here's a coloured kerchief for you,
> And also, a loaf of sweetbread!

But then his story of the sale of goods at market, and not necessarily a happy ending:

> This time I did well in Riga,
> I sold the flax profitably.
> To Melnbārdis. At that same place
> I sold the fabric, too.
> Only on Friday at the market
> Did I have trouble.
> The Devil knows!
> I was cheated of a third of the money
> Due to me for every pound of pork
> What a shame!
> It's so bad when you can't figure it out!
> And afterwards the boys in the shop
> Did seek to fleece me quite a lot;
> And when I wouldn't buy, then, like devils,
> They cursed me for a "bull's tail".
> They're deft at cheating and swindling
> And boxing the peasant's ears.

The experience has left Father with a bitter taste in his mouth, but he's determined that his eldest son, Juris, must be educated so that he will not be subject to the same mistreatment.

> Dear wife, Juris must be sent to school
> To learn to write and calculate.
> It seems to me he'll turn out bright;
> He'll manage to improve his mind.
> Through schooling one grows cleverer
> And in time becomes an honoured man!
> Let him learn to praise the Lord God

> And his holy faith;
>
> Let him learn the world's wily ways
>
> And the holy teaching of Jesus;
>
> Let him, thus rooted, become strong,
>
> So that his wisdom isn't doubted.

Ever the educator, like his brother and role model Andžs, Jānis emphasizes the honor that will come with the improvement of the mind.

And so, Jānis continues with this narrative poetry through Juris' various adventures and observations, all grounded in the Latvian country life that was his upbringing in the early 19th century. We experience "Juris' hardships as a shepherd" ('It's no laughing matter'), "Juris' delights as a shepherd" ('When I've done my shepherd's work/And put down my bag/I'm rewarded with/A tasty meal.') and "How juris, as a shepherd, sang of the beloved sun after a year at school." Travail, sacrifice, faith and endurance are cornerstones of these pastoral parables of the Piebalgan countryside.

Jānis inserts, too, a more worldly vignette, "A true story that Father told Juris," featuring a French orphan, Valentine, who suffers great hardship working in the fields but finally encounters great fortune in the teachings of the monk Brother Palemon. With his newfound education and greater work ethic, Valentine does a good deed for a traveling Englishman and is rewarded with the mentorship of German prince who is emperor of the city of Vienna and becomes his trusted assistant, living a long and fruitful life. To this father concludes:

> Now, my son Juris! You know
>
> The rewards for diligence,
>
> So, please remember this;
>
> Entrust your fortune to God,
>
> Who will know how you are doing?
>
> He remembers his people in time,

And draws unfortunates to himself,

He has the power to make happy and to scold!

Jānis' last vignette, "A good deed and a miserly reward," is short, the story of an honest peasant who finds a gentleman's purse filled with gold ducats and returns it, not expecting a reward. Though the gentleman insists on a miserly reward, Jānis notes

So should any Christian do without reward,

Whoever does not is placing shackles on his soul,

But a good deed should be rewarded with good;

That's lacking here, otherwise both would be commended.

"Story Songs" is at once didactic and instructive, and thoroughly characteristic of the country life in Jānis Rātminders' home of Vecpiebalga. He hoped to continue with further installments of his stories of Juris, concluding "Story Songs" with this message:

My friends, if these songs of mine

Should meet with your approval,

Then I'll dare to go on singing,

And tell more of Juris:

What a man he's become

And what good he's done.

Then I'll write down a second chapter,

Which will be superior to this.

In my spare time I'll happily seek

To gather more verses and sing even better.

This my mind is set on night and day,

To give my brothers what they need.

> God, let me experience
>
> From my countrymen this joy:
>
> That, both near and far,
>
> Their liking for book-reading should increase.
>
> Then the people's ignorance will end,
>
> And whoever writes will rejoice.

Though he was the subject of some praise and the collection sold in excess of 2,000 copies, historians don't give him much recognition for his work, certainly one of the earliest works of literature written in the Latvian language.

Certainly, the writings and reputations of Jānis Rātminders and his older brother Andžs Rātminders had an impact on those poets and novelists who followed, as evidenced by the work of Andrejs Pumpers and Matīss and Reinis Kaudzītes. Later still, the lyric poet Kārlis Skalbe (1879-1945) echoes the works of his Vecpiebalgan predecessors.

Jānis Rātminders lived most of his adult life in Riga and never returned to live in Vecpiebalga, but some speculation surrounds the possibility that his heart was broken by a childhood sweetheart. Still he expressed his fondness for home in one of his best-known poems, "Tomorrow, I'll Be Home No Longer" ("Rītu nebūšu vairs mājās"):

> Tomorrow I'll be home no longer
>
> The moment of parting is near.
>
> My legs already walk the path
>
> My thoughts remain right here.
>
> Climbing the hill over yonder
>
> I'll gaze back into the dale.
>
> I'll look down upon the place
>
> Where my joy once set sail.
>
> Then with my heart saddened

I'll continue to walk the line.
My beloved, though not beside me,
I'll hold forever in my mind.
But when the cold winter ends
A wondrous spring will be revived.
Then I can go forth again
And my legs will gladly oblige.
Then I'll happily return
To where love sings its song.
I'll begin a joyous new life,
And my sorrows will be gone.
And then on Midsummer's Eve
I'll adorn your door with birch leaves.
I'll pick flowers for you, my beloved
Through all the hills and valleys.

(Translation by Rihards Kalniņš)

The pastoral images and longing for the countryside of his home reappear with a dark tinge in Kārlis Skalbe's poetry. Not one to dwell in the drudgery of life, Skalbe was both an idealist and a dreamer. The anthologist W. K. Matthews notes that Skalbe "allows his interest in social matters to mingle with an idealism which expresses itself in simple imagery and floating patterns of music learnt from folk-song." His fairy tales of the countryside emphasize the closeness of man and nature and address adults more than children.

Late in life his longing for his homeland was the result of the political exile of his final years spent in Sweden. Homeland ("Dzimtene") reflects his desire to return to 'Saulkreiti' his home in Vecpiebalga overlooking Alauksts Lake, which the Second World War rendered unfulfilled.

Skalbe's earlier "Ever Blue Are the Latvian Hillsides" perhaps expresses best his love of this tragic land:

> Ever blue are the Latvian hillsides,
> Ever the Latvian birches murmur,
> Ever the zither weeps on the hillsides.
> All the votive vessels are shattered;
> Over the acres mists lie scattered;
> And under the forest's awning
> Wraiths flit from dimness to dawning.
> Ever white, the Daugava rapids
> Write on the stones their grizzled story;
> Never at rest are the Daugava rapids;
> Ever awake is the hero-heart.
> Ever blue are the Latvian hillsides,
> Ever the Latvian birches murmur,
> Ever the zither weeps on the hillsides.

Through the writings of my ancestor, Jānis Rātminders and the legacy of his brother Andžs Rātminders, and their association with the center of 19th Latvian culture in Piebalga, an appreciation for the greater canon of Latvian literature has grown to where the names Blaumanis and Skalbe and Jurjāns and Rainis and Alunāns and Azpazija and Ziedonis and Zālīte and many other Latvian writers and poets are as common to me as the American writers of my memory.

Chapter Eighteen

Latvian Relatives!

Certainly, I had no expectation of finding relatives, no matter how distant, when I first visited Latvia. My grandparents and father (aged 3) were the last in our family to see Augusta Rathminder Maddaus' sisters, Marija Johanna (Marie) and Eizenija Antonija (Jenny), when they extended granddad's business trip to Berlin for a visit to Riga, then still part of the Russian Empire. Two of the few photos of my father from his early years were taken in the Berlin Zoo and the sisters' backyard in Agenkalns, Riga, with a note on the latter--" Tante Jenny, 1912." The house at Skolas iela 39 (39 Woodcock Street) was built by Jānis Rātminders in 1880, the year of his death. I am not clear if it was completed before he died or whether he actually lived in it but he was buried across the street in Martina kapi (Martin's Cemetery). It should be noted that some records including her passport suggest Marija lived at Slokas iela 23, but as far as I can tell, the address was renumbered to Slokas iela 39 during the interbellum period of the Latvian Republic.

According to Riga's St. Johns Church records, Marie, Jānis' wife, died in 1909 at the age of 84, and their eldest son Heinrich in 1919 at age 72. The surviving sisters, Marija and Antonija, apparently took in boarders for income. At one point in the late 1920s, Augusta and her son Ingo, Sr. made a failed court attempt to recognize her interest in the property, but by then the Latvian judicial system would not agree to the legal move.

Antonija was the only one of the two to marry, to a widower named Friemanis and they lived for a time in Minsk. His death is recorded in 1894 and subsequent census listings include his daughter Anna as well as the sisters. Antonija died in 1937 at age 81, the same year as her sister Augusta, leaving Marija as the surviving family member.

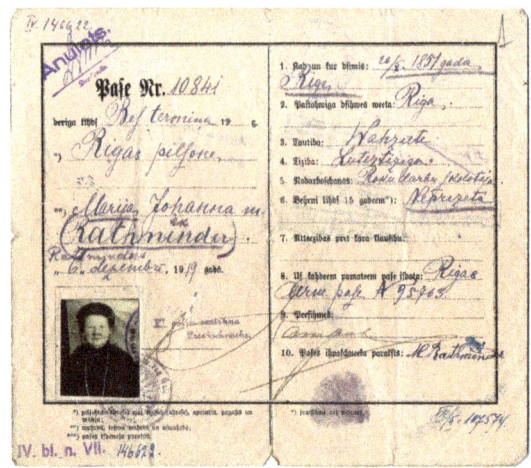

Marija Rathminder's Latvian Passport, issued 1919

After the Soviets invaded Latvia in 1940, Marija suffered a two-pronged indignity in her 90th year with both events listed in archival records. On January 22, 1941, hers was one of hundreds of apartments and boarding houses taken by the Soviets, effectively eliminating the individual ownership and the 'oppression' of the bourgeois class. Later that spring, in an agreement with the Nazis, Marija was one of over 2,700 Rigans identified as ethnic German--due to her preference of the German language--to be repatriated to Western Poland.

At age 90, and after 60 years of living in the home her father built, Marija was transported by train to Poland. No trace of her was documented once she left Riga. I can only imagine the difficulties she faced and the disjointed sense of despair she must have felt leading up to her certain, imminent death.

Dad's Uncle Oscar had the occasion to attend ecumenical meetings in Europe after the Second World War in his role as pastor of the Manhasset Reformed Church and he took the opportunity to travel behind the Iron Curtain to Riga, but found no living relatives. He visited the home of Tante Marie and Tante Jenny and was greeted with a gift of items such as napkin rings and table cloths that belonged to the sisters. The current residents of the house told him they kept the items because they knew that someday family would come to visit them.

Of course, it came as a big surprise to me to be introduced to Lelde and he mother Anda in 2010. We had come to believe with some certainty that we had no living relatives in Latvia, that the wars and the Soviet occupation had all but eliminated any possibility of surviving kin.

But maybe I shouldn't have been so surprised. From the time we returned from our 2009 visit to Latvia and through to the following spring, I had been unearthing evidence of 19th Century Rātminders family births, marriages and deaths in the digitized records of the Vecpiebalga church in hopes of finding Augusta Dorothea Rathminder. I found her later in the Riga St. John's church records, but by that time I had generated a list of uncles, aunts, cousins, nieces and nephews that was overwhelming. In addition to our ancestor Jānis, his brothers Andžs, Jēkabs and Matīss and sister Anna Korneta were among other things, family oriented and they were blessed with descendants to carry on the family Augusta was but one of 25 first cousins born of the children of Andžs and Marija Rathminder of the Zeikari farmstead. That none of their progeny would be alive today is really hard to believe when you think of it.

The serendipity with which I discovered our living relatives in itself was also really not that remarkable. An English teacher with decades of service in the Vecpiebalga secondary school would more than likely have taught one or more of our relatives. The only truly unexpected twist may have been that Mirdza and Anda knew each other before Mirdza came to teach there.

Since our initial meeting, Lelde has introduced me to her sister and brother, uncle and aunt, and numerous cousins, nieces and nephews. And many of those have introduced me to other relatives. Most are descendants of Jēkabs Rātminders and as far as I know, none of the other 4 original Zeikari children have living descendants. But I have an open mind on this, based on past experience.

The Rātminders surname has faded from existence, as far as I can tell. One of the last 'Zeikari' Rātminders, also named Jānis Rātminders, died in October of 1938 at age 94. I also found mention of a Kārlis Rātminders who may have lived into the 1940s, the records are not clear as far as he is concerned. In any case the surname has disappeared and relatives with the names of Ozola, Avena, Šlesere, Zariņš, Snips, Avots, and others carry on the family traits.

From the first meeting, I became interested in how these relatives managed to survive the 20th century, with all its turbulence and destruction, but understanding that Soviet times enforced a special sort of stoicism, I was careful not to ask too many questions. For some families, the Second World War had tragic implications. For others, who might consider themselves 'not very important,' survival was a daily routine, until independence came in 1991.

Lelde once again provided the opening I needed to understand their histories. During a gathering at her Aunt Māra's home before a Song Festival dance event, she explained that the apartment had belonged to her grandparents. I knew by then of her grandfather, Harijs Avens, a well-known movie actor, and had seen a compilation video made by Lelde's brother Kriss which included many clips of his acting. The conversation moved between Lelde's explanation of the event to follow and introductions to the various relatives that came in and out, including Lelde's friends from Siberia. She transitioned almost flawlessly between her native Latvian to English for our benefit and Russian for her friends.

After mention of her grandparents and especially her grandmother, Skaidrīte (Sipols) Avena, whose family originally lived there, I asked the question that I had been wanting to ask for some time: "How did they survive the War and the occupation?" Lelde, being a professional historian and a constant teacher of all things Latvian where I am concerned, began to explain, with numerous questions and corrections from Anda and her Aunt Māra. Before too long, among the cacophony of conversation in the room, she laid out the intriguing story of Harijs and Skaidrīte which I will include below. Beth and I were fascinated with this singular historical thread which winds its way through the Soviet occupation of independent Latvia in 1940, the Nazi invasion of 1941, the Soviet return in 1944 and the post-War 'Soviet times.'

Soon it was time to leave for the Dance performance in nearby Daugava Stadium, which we thoroughly enjoyed, but we carried with us the memory of Lelde's remarkable family history. I was determined not to forget this history but upon return home to the US and with a two-year gap between visits to Latvia, the details became, understandably, fuzzy.

Returning in 2015 with my brother John and cousin Bill and his wife Linda, I made it a point to arrange a meeting with Lelde as this would be their first time in Latvia, and first occasion to meet our relatives there. Lelde, as usual, made the extra effort to welcome us and arranged for a family gathering in Jelgava, southwest of Riga, where her sister Anete lived with her husband Arturs and son Reinalds. Anete and Lelde took us on a short boat cruise on the Lielupe River, a tour of the grounds of Jelgava Castle, a walk through a remarkable sand sculpture exhibit, and a climb up an observation tower to see the cityscape. We then were treated to a beautiful dinner at Anete's house outside the city. Anda and Māra and Krišs (the first I had met him), as well as other cousins made the dinner quite an event!

Family Photo at Jelgava Castle

On our return to Riga, seated in the backseat of a van Gatis had borrowed to transport us to Jelgava, I got out a notepad and asked Lelde to retell her family's history, ostensibly for my brother John's benefit. Once again, we were spellbound by the story, but I tried to made sure to take copious notes.

What follows is the result of my notes, what I was able to glean from hearing Lelde's story of her grandparents along with a few notes Lelde provided in later correspondence. I have included some additional historical research of my own.

Lelde has since sent a more detailed and researched version of the story, much of which enriches the story of their relationship and the historical context of their life. I'm hoping that she could publish it someday on its own.

Harijs and Skaidrīte Avens

The heartbreaking stories of Latvians dispersed during Soviet and Nazi occupations of World War Two, and the extended Soviet occupation that came in the aftermath of the War, range from the Siberian deportations of June 14, 1941, to the Nazi Waffen conscriptions of the middle years of the War, to the Russian Gulag imprisonments, to the exile of Latvians refugees to Sweden, Germany and other locations in advance of the final Soviet advance of late 1944 and early 1945. Few of these stories combine as many of these scenarios as that of Harijs and Skaidrīte Avens and their young family. Theirs is one of determination, human dignity, loyalty and, and above all, love.

Harijs and Skaidrīte married in 1938 with little inkling of the sinister signing of the Molotov-Ribbentrop Treaty to be executed by the Nazis and Soviets a year later. In effect, this secret agreement divided the whole of Eastern Europe in two, giving Germany the impetus to invade Poland on September 9, 1939 and leading to the Soviet Annexation of Estonia, Latvia, and Lithuania in 1940. For the newlyweds, the terrible history that would ravage their beloved Latvia was unthinkable.

Latvia in 1938 was a small country, 18 years in existence and enjoying independence and modest economic prosperity in spite of the interwar depression. The ethnic Latvians had risen out of the ashes of World War I, repelled the Bolshevik threat of the new Soviet state, and achieved what had been the long-awaited and dreamed-of goal of their mid-19th century National Awakening.

Indeed, the young couple had been born as subjects of Tsar Nicholas II and the Russian Empire, Skaidrīte in Riga in 1914, Harijs in rural Vecpiebalga, four years earlier. From the ages of roughly 6 and 10 respectively, they had thrived in the culture and the opportunity reflected by the growth of the new nation. Both pursued advanced studies at the University of Latvia, Harijs in Economics and Accounting, Skaidrīte in Law. And both were active in the arts, as Harijs gained a foothold as an actor in the National Theatre while Skaidrīte sang in the choir. When a choir was required for one Theatre production, they were involved and perhaps their fates were sealed.

Harijs Avens (10/21/1910--12/25/1976) came to Riga from the Piebalga region of Central Vidzeme, east of the capital. His parents, Peteris and Marija, worked the farmstead in Greiveri, not far from the village of Vecpiebalga. Harijs's maternal grandmother, Made, was the daughter of Jēkabs Rātminders of the Zeikari farmstead and one of 25 cousins, who included Līze Ratmindere Kaudzite and Augusta Dorothea Rathminder Maddaus, our great-grandmother. Made's Uncle Andžs was the longtime 19th century teacher of the Vecpiebalga Parish school and her Uncle Jānis (our great, great grandfather) was a teacher in Riga, and well-known poet. Harijs traveled to Riga in the late 1920s to follow his desire to both act and study at the University. His involvement in the National Theatre led to a role in the first full-length Latvian movie with sound, "The Fisherman's Son," in 1939.

151

Skaidrīte's family, the Sipols, had settled in Riga before her birth and her father made his living building water pumps and moving freight. Born Skaidrīte Ziedone Vilma Sipols, (5/23/1914--10/01/1988) she was the youngest of 4 sisters--by 7 years--attractive, with a beautiful singing voice and keen intellect. At University, participation in the sorority Varavīksne had very great impact of Skaidrīte's life She was very active in social life there. Inside Varavīksne they had almost 200 members till 1940. For some semesters Skaidrīte was a leader of sorority Varavīksne.

With Soviet annexation of Latvia in 1940 came the never-ending task of coping with the invading forces while struggling to maintain a semblance of normalcy in day-to-day living. Before the WWII, the Molotov-Ribbentrop pact was signed and Latvia – USSR cooperation agreement also took place, in the Spring of 1939 Latvia made additional mobilization in Latvian Army and Harijs was mobilized there till the Occupation of Latvia and little longer September 1940. So, he clearly realized what happened with his country.

Fortunately, the immediate family was spared the deportations of June 14th and any mortal harm. Harijs and Skaidrīte continued their studies as much as they could, with Harij earning his accounting degree in 1942 and Skaidrīte, having already finished her Latvian Law studies and working in a law office, setting out to learn the USSR legal system recently put in place, such as it was.

With 1941 and 1942, came two significant changes for the young couple. Firstly, in mid-1941, Hitler broke trust with Stalinist Russia, and the German army pushed the Soviets out of the Baltics and to the gates of the Kremlin. Secondly, and more happily, came the arrival in 1942 of the couple's first child, and what a tumultuous time for Anda to arrive! Harijs was able to work as an accountant in the Ostland government while Skaidrīte was home with Anda, and soon a second child, Āris, made his appearance. But the Nazi occupation was tenuous at best, and soon the hope that Latvian independence might be restored with the help of the Germans became a fading dream. Cooperating with the occupiers became one more acting role for Harijs and his family, and the role would continue in one form or another for the rest of his life.

Supported by supply convoys from the West through Archangel (Russian Arctic Seaport) and set with a resolve to not accept defeat, the Soviet army began to turn the tide against the weary Nazi invaders, and in 1944, the Soviets began to take extreme measures to maintain their goals in the region. The locals gritted their teeth, powerless to deal with the disintegrating Nazi force and the effect of their imminent withdrawal.

Ultimately, able-bodied Latvian men were conscripted into the Latvian Legion, a division of the Nazi Waffen SS. These divisions were in direct breach of the 1907 Hague Convention which prohibited enlistment of citizens into the occupation military. The first Latvians, more than 80,000 in number, born in 1919-1924, were sent in 1943 to the Russian Front, where many lost their lives in battle. Harijs became a member, against his will, of the 15th Division of the Legion, a smaller group made up of conscripts born between 1908-1926 and later expanded to 1906-1928. He was shipped to Poland to participate in work details near the city of Torun, the birthplace of Nicolaus Copernicus, and the capital of the Pomeranian Province. These troops were ostensibly the Ostarbeiter, or Eastern, 'guest workers,' but they were also being trained to return to the front, although they may have been involved in more forced-labor than training. They were primarily 'ditch diggers' in Pomerania in early March 1945, and with dwindling numbers, were sent in April to the 'Courland Pocket' in western Latvia to serve as the last force in the Baltics against the Soviet Army. Harijs was taken as a prisoner of war by Soviets near Ventspils in Kurzeme (Courland), in the middle of May 1945

Harijs was transferred to an NKVD filtration camp in Dubrovka, to the east, southeast of St. Petersburg. This had been the site of one of the bloodiest fronts of World War II, as Soviet troops met the retreating Nazi army across the river from Dubrovka at Nevsky Pyatachok, resulting in combined casualties of over 400,000 soldiers over an 18-month period. The NKVD was the law enforcement agency of the Soviet Union, which eventually was split into the Ministry of Internal Affairs and the KGB, or secret police. The NKVD filtration, or silence camps were prisoner of war camps or gulags, designed by the Soviet secret police to screen former citizens of Soviet territories which had previously been held by the Germans, mostly as forced laborers. As a former Nazi Waffen soldier, this put Harijs' loyalties in question and he spent a year proving his value to his Soviet captors. Heaven only knows what the conditions and duties of the captives consisted of.

Many in the filtration camps starved to death, but Harijs was able to survive for a variety of reasons. One, he was multilingual and spoke fluent Russian. Two, his accounting skills were valuable in the camp and he was cooperative in lending his talents. Three, though he was paid in cigarettes, he was not a smoker and traded his pay for additional food. And four, he was a large man and in effect, lived off his body fat. On June 12, 1946, he was released. After a year in the camp, he was deemed suitable for return to the Soviet society in the occupied Latvian Soviet Socialist Republic, and returned to Riga and the home of his in-laws.

With Harijs a part of the Waffen SS, Skaidrīte made the difficult decision to leave Riga with Anda and Āris and boarded a ship on October 2, 1944 from Riga to Danzig, Poland. Although under different circumstances, the couple may have passed close to each other in Poland, as Skaidrīte made her way by land to the Czech Republic, moving ever westward ahead of the Soviet front. It would be months before they would see each other again, and only after a number of miraculous turns in their travels. In Amberg, she worked like the agricultural laborer, as a helper in farm till the end of WWII. In June 1945, she was responsible for young girl scouts, and she filled this role later in Wurzburg DP Camp, too.

Skaidrīte and the children found refuge in the Wurzburg DP (Displaced Persons) Camp in the American sector of occupied Germany and stayed for most of 1945-47. Located on the Main River and midway between Frankfort and Nuremburg in Northern Bavaria, Wurzburg was one of a number of German cities which was fire-bombed during the latter stages of the war. some accounts suggest the bombing of Wurzburg was even more extensive than that of Dresden, a month before. After the War, the Wurzburg DP Camp became one of the largest of its kind, with a population ranging between 2,500-5,000, consisting of mostly Estonians, Ukrainians and Latvians. Skaidrīte worked here as a helper in the hospital, as a nurse.

The DP Camps were a sort of limbo for many, as noted by the commentary of one Latvian, Ilmars Bergmanis:

> And I don't know what there is to tell about the DP camps. There was very little to eat, a little better in the American Zone than in English and French because Americans were more generous distributing the army surplus. We were poorly clothed. We were longing to go back home to Latvia but one very positive thing about the DP camps was that we lived in those camps like in a small Latvia.
>
> We had our own schools, our own church service, fraternal life was flourishing, nobody had to learn German, because we didn't have to go outside the gates and there was no need to wander outside. We didn't need them and they didn't need us. Everybody basically was happy in the camps with empty stomachs and nobody had to worry about diet and exercises. And nobody wanted to go back to Latvia either.
>
> So - we were just sitting 5 years and waiting till America, Australia, England and Canada will start calling and by 1949 they started calling: Australia wanted to take whole families no matter how many people in the family and what condition. England took only single males who can work in coal mines; Canada basically wanted only young and middle-aged women who could work in households and America wanted only families who could work right away and who could get world church organizations affidavits. And United States only took 200,000 Balts, special legislature signed in Congress. (http://www.dpcamps.org/balts.html)

For Skaidrīte, Anda and Aris, the outcome was as uncertain as for the rest of the residents of the camp, but the wait turned out to be shorter. Soviet propaganda radio broadcasts included messages from Riga encouraging relatives to return to Latvia. One day (May 22 1947), someone in the camp heard on a broadcast that Harijs was still alive in Riga and passed the information on to Skaidrīte. At first this information was doubted, but gave her hope and eventually she was able to verify Harijs' situation. (She wrote a letter to him on February 1947 and received reply on October 1947.) And so, she was left to make an anguishing and pivotal decision. Wait for the call from one of the Western countries for a permanent move to freedom, or return to her husband and the father of her children in Soviet-occupied Latvia. Freedom or love and family. The choice was fraught with uncertainty. Each choice had its benefits and downsides.

In November of 1947, Skaidrīte made her choice and after days of travel, she and the children were reunited with Harijs, in Riga, on December 9th, 1947. There, they stayed and determined to make a life under the oppressive Soviet regime. Joyfully, Māra was born in 1948, expanding the family to five.

Having earned a supporting acting role in one movie, "Zvejnieka dēls" ("The Fisherman's Son," 1939) and acted in the Latvian National Theatre, Harijs turned to acting to support the family. His acting career became a long and successful one, with 19 acting credits (IMDb), mostly between 1948 and 1972. He also continued his accounting career while Skaidrīte worked in a market on Brivibas iela (street) selling milk products from the kolkhoz in the countryside. After the death of Stalin in 1953, she was able to secure a position in a bookstore which specialized in works on national politics. She moved to the bookstore's new location in 1960 and retired with a pension in 1975. Harijs died the next year at Christmastime, having lived a complicated and difficult life, having seen so many of his countrymen succumb to the ravages of war.

Skaidrīte continued to anchor her family until her death in 1988. She died not long after her son-in-law, Valters Ozols, (Anda's husband) died at the age of 46. Lelde feels that Skaidrīte's illness was because of suppressed emotions, trying always be nice, polite, what she really was. But for everybody there are minutes or moments that you are angry or not satisfied with something – that all stayed in her deep corners of inner life.

The children--Anda, Āris and Māra--who had not known independence in Latvia, observed their parents with consternation and stoicism. But they also know that their mere existence and survival of the difficult Soviet Times is a testament to the love shared by Harijs and Skaidrīte Avens.

Lelde later wrote to me with the following coda to her story:

> "Harijs and Skaidrīte really loved each other! I am grateful them that they stayed/returned in Latvia. They brought traditions and also ability of free thinking and speaking through the Soviet times! Only there was a price of that – Harijs and Skaidrīte took that hard burden on themselves. I am thankful that I can be here in my father and mother land and do what I consider meaningful. I know that my mom, Āris and Māra couldn't be so free inside, with their own opinion and in that mean time acceptable to another point of view, and so friendly, if their parents would be different."

Each family history of course is different and while plenty of generalizations can be made about the fate of Latvians resulting from the Molotov-Ribbentrop Agreement, the Second World War and the Soviet Occupation, for Americans the history is not too well known. We do know that a certain portion of the Latvian population became refugees in Western Europe, eventually settling in the United Kingdom, Australia, the U.S., Canada and other 'western' countries which would take them. Through the writing of Aleksandr Solzhenitsyn and a few others, we also knew of the horrors of the gulag system in Soviet Russia and the fact that many behind the Iron Curtain were relocated to Siberia and other territories in the USSR. The details were largely uncovered by American press, if I could make that assertion. The American stance became one of opposition to the spread of communism and Soviet Russia became one of our greatest existential threats in the world, at least until the fall of the Berlin Wall in 1989.

Soviet oppression of Latvia, once it began in 1940, came in many forms, but is often best characterized by the deportations of June 1941--just before the Nazi invasion of the Baltics--and March of 1949, as a measure of Stalin's frustration with Latvian's unwillingness to fully submit to collectivization of farms and industry after the War. Thousands of Latvians, Estonians and Lithuanians were packed on cattle cars during these two events and deported to interior Russia. Most were from the intellectual class, civil servants, or former government officials. The men were sent to the gulags, most never to be seen again, and the women and children were sent to remote Siberian villages to live in starvation and squalor. Only a few of the latter group returned after Stalin's death allowed for it.

One of a number of accounts of these deportations that I have found most compelling was "With Dance Shoes in Siberian Snows" by Sandra Kalniete, the story of her parents' deportation in 1949. She was born in Siberia in 1952 and although her father and grandmother did not survive, she and her mother were eventually able to return to Latvia. Kalniete has lived a remarkable life that includes involvement in the Popular Front movement of the late 1980s, serving as a member of Saiema, the Latvian parliament and later as a member of European parliament. That she came from such a difficult background with such overwhelming odds is just one of the many stories of Latvian perseverance that characterizes all three Baltic republics. Fortunately, it's also a story that has been translated to English and numerous other languages, making the Latvian occupation story accessible to people all over the world.

Similar stories are undoubtedly found in many Latvian families, whether they have been published as Kalniete's has been, or recorded by our cousin Lelde in video testimonies kept in the records of the Occupation Museum of Latvia in Riga. Each story is different with different destinations and tragic twists and all reflect the tortured history of a country in the crossfire of larger, more powerful neighbors.

One of our relatives, has a story similar to Kalniete's. In his Latvian language memoir, "Klejojumi" (literally, "Wanderings"), Arturs Snips shares the story of his birth in Siberia in 1949 and 'return' to Latvia in 1957. Grandfather sent to the gulag due to his involvement in the Piebalgan militia, mother and grandmother sent to Siberia, Arturs' birth and return to Latvia, like Kalniete, Arturs' life is one marked by the turmoil in the Baltics. And like Kalniete, he became involved in the Third Awakening events that led to Latvian re-independence.

Trained as an engineer, Arturs teamed with journalist Dainis Īvāns to produce a remarkable essay during the latter years of Soviet rule. The subject was a hydroelectric dam to be constructed on the upper reaches of the Daugava River near Daugavpils, which, like the Rigas HES hydro project in Salaspils, would flood much of the valley and its uniqueness. Popular opinion, though not generally allowed under Soviet rule, was nonetheless beginning to be tolerated by the Gorbachev government and its policies of glasnost and perestroika.

In "Imagining the Nation: History, Modernity, and Revolution in Latvia," Daina Stukuls Eglitis recounts the sequence of events:

> In 1986, the Daugava again became the site of a struggles that, while not itself of epic proportions, was a catalyst in the mass Latvian mobilization against Soviet power, which ended in the defeat of the Soviet regime in Latvia and arguable contributed to the collapse of the empire itself, an epic conclusion to be sure. The struggle began with an article in the progressive weekly newspaper *Literatura un maksla* (Literature and Art): the piece, written by the journalist Dainis Īvāns and the engineer Arturs Snips, was a critique of Soviet plans to build a hydroelectric station (HES) on the Daugava River in southeastern Latvia. The writers deplored the lack of expertise and bureaucratic incompetence of those responsible for the project, suggesting that the damming of the Daugava would flood the surrounding arable land and forests and worsen pollution problems. The writers also invoked the spirit of Latvian national consciousness, reiterating the significance of the Daugava in Latvian culture, and writing that "We cannot allow technicians to determine single-handedly the future of our common home, our river of destiny."

A groundswell of popular opposition led not only to the Latvian Council of Ministers returning a negative evaluation of the project in early 1987 and later that year the USSR Council of Ministers halted the project.

Not only did the issue lead to the nixing the project, but it mobilized public sentiment around the establishment of the Latvian Popular Front with Īvāns, Kalniete and others as its leaders. Peaceful protest typified in this issue, the Singing Revolution and the Baltic Way all contributed to the reestablishment of Latvian independence in 1991. While not the political leader Īvāns became, Arturs Snips' contribution to the effort must not be underestimated. He continues to write and philosophize on a variety of topics to this day.

While we in the Western world mark the collapse of the Soviet Union with President Reagan's "Mr. Gorbachev, tear down that wall" speech, the Solidarity movement in Poland and the ultimate fall of the Berlin Wall in November of 1989, those in the Baltics know that their concerted, peaceful efforts were equally instrumental in the demise of the USSR and more importantly in their rightful freedom from communist oppression. For Latvians, Estonians and Lithuanians, World War Two did not end in 1945, it ended in 1991.

It's been fascinating to see Latvian history and culture through the 20th Century stories of Harijs Avens and Arturs Snips as well as the 19th century biographies of Jānis Rātminders and Johann Karl Ludwig Maddaus, but my window into Latvia has also been expanded through the efforts of Lelde and Gatis, as I've mentioned earlier in this text, but also a larger and larger group of relatives, more with each year and each visit.

I've seen Kolkarags, Slitere National Park, and Ventspils with Arturs' daughter Arta, visited Anita and Raimonds at their farmstead in Jaungreiveri on the shores of Alauksts ezers near Vecpiebalga, walked the beach in Jurmala in the late light of June night with Anita's son Viesturs and his friend Inese, walked the historic Riga cemeteries with Māra and her grandchildren Rihards and Una, traveled to Saldus, Kuldiga and Broceni--walking across the iconic Venta rumba (reputed to be the widest in Europe, although only 3-4 meters high) in Kuldiga--with Kārlis and Liga, walked the many levels of the Latvian National Library with Beatē and toured the impressive family farm of the Avots family in Bauska.

Each and every time I visit Latvian relatives, I learn more about the country and its qualities and each and every time I'm enveloped in their gracious hospitality. I really can't imagine feeling more welcome, and yet each time I visit, I feel more welcome.

Chapter Nineteen

The Life of the Village, and the Life of the Quest

> Well, my friend said to me
> I guess it's all history
> You ever wonder
> What might have happened if you stayed?
> I said there's the life of the village
> And the life of the quest
> And we both went our separate ways.
> (Barney Bentall/Cory Tetford)

Looking over the generations from Georg Maddaus in Hamburg to Johann Karl Ludwig Maddaus in Hamburg and Riga, Oscar W. Maddaus in Riga and Brooklyn and my grandfather Ingo in Brooklyn, I am fascinated with the lives they led. How much of their lives involved 'wanderlust?' How much of their lives involved the life of the village and how much involved the life of the quest? When they moved, what propelled them?

Georg died at 23 and other than the fact that he was a 'painter' and a few statistics about his family, we know little about him. Perhaps he had a family at such a young age that a quest was not possible or he just preferred the closeness of his family and the community he grew up in. We will never know.

Having his father die at age 2 or 3 set a different course for Johann and his siblings. A move with his mother and stepfather to Frohse in the vicinity of Magdeburg, away from his paternal home of Hamburg, must certainly have shaped his future, if not the fact that as a young man, the Prussian Army was beckoning. An artistic and entrepreneurial soul, his move to Hanseatic Riga followed his spiritual calling. But for the next 38 years until his death, Riga became his home and only occasional tours of Western Europe interrupted his life there. He seemed to thrive in Riga, with no desire to leave.

Oscar Wilhelm shared some of his father's artistic talents, and as time went on his was a life of the quest. Moving to America in the late 1860s, he established himself as a commercial artist, but seemed driven by the desire to achieve the unachievable while constantly trying to out-run his financial and familial responsibilities. His multiple crossings of the Atlantic from Riga to New York and back were at times characterized by the desire to engage in import/export markets and he was active in selling goods made in America to buyers in the Russian Empire. One note from Uncle Oscar on the back of a postcard of St. Peter's Church suggested his father represented International Harvester in Russia. Oscar Wilhelm at one time proposed a rail crossing of the Bering Strait to New York investors, but his resources and methods never appeared to be up to the task.

Ingo, Sr., our grandfather, enjoyed the life of the Wall Street import/export markets, not far removed from one of his father's talents, and in spite of the 20th century's two world wars and depression, he died a relatively successful man. His life was characterized by his immersion in New York's Wall Street district and a reserved but close relationship with his mother and siblings. He traveled at times when his income allowed, mostly to Germany on business. His goal in life was typified by his last residence in the comfortable--and now high-priced--neighborhood of Brooklyn Heights in a 3rd floor apartment with a dramatic view of lower Manhattan across the East River. And his surviving sisters Freida and Senta lived in apartments of their own close by.

Our father, Ingo, Jr. was brought up during one of the successful periods of Ingo, Sr.'s import/export business, in Park Slope, Brooklyn and

Russell Gardens, Great Neck, NY and had entered Columbia University by the time the Great Depression obliterated his father's business. He never talked much about the latter period, mentioning once he never knew how his parents survived the Great Depression, and seemed to be more concerned with intellectual pursuits of a Mathematics professor, taking care of his family and discovering new parts of the American Wilderness. He did not settle in Upstate New York until the age of 38 but that became his home until his death at 95.

The quests of these patriarchs of our family varied a great deal and transcended the concern for family history as such but I am not satisfied that they were the only factors in our loss of connection with our Baltic German and Latvian heritage. Others have emigrated from Latvia and maintained their strong connections to the culture and language and some have returned to become active members of the Latvian citizenry.

This can be chalked up to a number of factors, I guess, and one study "The Emigrant Communities of Latvia: National Identity, Transnational Relations, and Diaspora Politics," in which 14,068 Latvian emigrants were surveyed in 118 countries by University of Latvia Sociologist Inta Mieriņa suggests that immigrant experience can cover the entire spectrum of attitude towards the homeland. Mieriņa surveyed expatriate Latvians in mid 2010s United Kingdom and found that equal parts considered themselves assimilated with no desire to return home, others felt they were European and could move back and forth with ease, and another third retained their Latvian identities and fully intended to return to Latvia at some point in the not-so-distant future.

It's not unexpected that this partition of Latvians in America would not be similar, and with our family an added factor was the combination of Baltic German and Latvian heritage. It seems the latter fell away the quickest. Augusta Dorothea may never had identified as Latvian in spite of her father's love and advancement of the culture in his writing and teaching. She spoke German solely throughout her life and learned little English in her final 50 years in America. We don't know if she ever spoke Latvian (or Russian), but neither seems important in her life, in spite of having a father who was so involved and impassioned about establishing the Latvian language in intellectual circles.

Grandfather was the bridge, certainly, from the Old World to America. He was bilingual and had a robust business dependent on his bilingual skills, when the economy would allow. His generation became American but retained German language skills as well and seemed to flow between the two effortlessly, if only for their closeness to their mother.

The clean break from our German heritage came with my father. He resisted the language to the point of failing a required course in German at Columbia and only meeting the requirement in 'Technical German,' whatever that was. I have this concept of a Math course with directions in German, but might be wrong on that count. He never mentioned it and I only discovered it on his University transcript after his death. And so, he willingly became assimilated in American culture, including his love of baseball--the New York Yankees in particular after the Dodgers betrayed Brooklyn for LA--travel to distant parts of America, including Baxter State Park in Maine early in its existence and Alaska not long after the ALCAN highway was completed. He always had a fascination with numbers and to some degree, the English language. Not a flag waving patriot, he worked on the radar project in Building 20 at MIT during the end of the Second World War, making his contribution to this vital war effort.

Dad was somewhat of a stoic with a sensitive underside and I have come to believe--perhaps not accurately--that he also wanted to feel 100 percent American for defensive reasons, not unlike many second-generation American children of immigrants. Identifying as German during the First World War and the interbellum period was beyond his comfort zone, and I do not blame him.

German culture flourished in America from the time of the vast 19th century migration up to the beginning of the 20th century, only to be largely eradicated with the onset of World War I. Over one-tenth of Americans in 1900 could trace their ancestry to Germany and German culture was omnipresent through much of the country. Oscar Wilhelm Maddaus came to America around 1870 that was bursting with German culture and it is no wonder he moved so freely within the economy. Ingo, Sr. was able to thrive in the maelstrom of early 20th century foreign trade, bringing German machinery and technology to a rapidly growing America.

World War I changed everything. As Erik Kirschbaum outlines in "Burning Beethoven: The Eradication of German Culture in the United States during World War I," the once vibrant German-American heritage was scapegoated for the acts of Imperial Germany. With the onset of the War in 1914, British propaganda efforts made it clear that Kaiser Wilhelm II would do anything to ensure German victory. The sinking of the Lusitania in 1915 and the German "Rape of Belgium" early in the War served to outrage Britain and America alike and the Zimmerman telegram of January 1917 all but cemented American distrust of anyone or anything German. The coded telegram to the German ambassador in Washington, among other things, disclosed a German plan to propose an alliance with Mexico and Mexican invasion of the United States.

Germans were suspected of being spies, or German agents, German-American leaders were sent to internment camps, and firing squads were widely recommended for traitors. In 1918, a German immigrant named Robert Paul Prager--who had once tried to join the US Navy and also was denied coal miner union membership--was lynched in southern Illinois, just outside of St. Louis. Kirschbaum notes: "Prager was only one part of more than thirty Germans killed in vigilante attacks in the United States during World War I, yet his hanging death epitomizes that dark and long-forgotten era of United States history, when anti-German hysteria swept across the country." While President Wilson won reelection in 1916 in part by pledging to keep America out of the War, the overwhelming sentiment against Germans accelerated by the Zimmerman telegram led to Congressional approval of American entry in 1917.

In 1900, about one in ten Americans were ethnic German and

concentrations of Germans were found in major cities such as Chicago (with the sixth largest German population in the world at the time) and small towns from Pennsylvania to Texas to Wisconsin and Missouri, and virtually every state in-between. Interestingly, Prohibition was finally passed in 1917 using a largely anti-German model, where other previous attempts had failed.

New York City, the home of the Maddaus family from 1883, was in 1900, the second largest in the world in terms of ethnic German population. Only Berlin in Germany had more. More than a quarter of New York's 3.5 million residents were either of German birth or had one or more parents who were. German culture thrived up until the War, when it nearly vanished. The War and the associated events leading to it made it dangerous to be German, and the once chauvinistic culture shriveled to non-existence.

It is not as if 8 million German-Americans disappeared as a result of the War, but most if not all ceased identifying as German and became American solely, in a purely defensive posture. For Augusta Rathminder Maddaus, now in her late 60s, this meant further isolation due to her lack of English language skills and for her children, mostly in their late 30s and early 40s, it meant keeping their heads down and speaking only English in public, while continuing on the routines of their established vocations and speaking German mostly in their mother's home. Ingo, Sr. would perhaps be the only sibling to continue using German in his work, although certainly German imports slowed to a trickle with War raging.

For Ingo, Jr., born in 1909, and to some extent his younger brother Paul, three years his junior, the turn of public sentiment against anything and anyone German must certainly have had its effect. I have no doubt that my father's desire to be 100 percent American and his aversion to the German language was established during his adolescence, as America prepared for and fought the First World War. As much as he loved his Grandmother, she was probably the only thing German he would endure. Uncle Paul would dabble in genealogy to the point where he would determine that our family tree included Latvians but apparently my father would have none of it and conversation of our ancestors rarely if ever included ethnicity.

So, my quest over the past ten years has been to reconstruct the family history, as much as is possible. If anything, I've learned you cannot generalize about one's history based on their family history. I also know that it all becomes complicated when I add in the Meade and Willis heritage from my paternal grandmother's family, and the Raymonds--back to Salem, Massachusetts in the 1640s--and the Behringers and McBrides and Allens from my mother's family--English and Scotch-Irish and even more Germans, and maybe even some Scandinavian blood from one side or the other.

That Latvian ancestors play such a big part in my search belies their contribution to my makeup. Jānis Rātminders represents only one of 16 great, great grandparents and the only ethnic Latvian. Perhaps some study of genetic markers and DNA might suggest I received more from him than the other 15, or maybe less, I do not know. Tracing back to his family and farmstead in Zeikari, near the village of Vecpiebalga, Latvia has been fascinating to me and has justified the journey.

Chapter Twenty

Oscar Wilhelm Maddaus
(1845-1896)
Artist, Musician, Importer

Oscar Wilhelm Maddaus, c. 1880 in Riga

Oscar Wilhelm is probably the most enigmatic of our ancestors and the least mentioned in our family over the years I was growing up. Even the slightest detail about him, for instance what the "W." stood for, was not passed along and most if not all of what I share here is from public records. He managed to pass from the family memory.

Oscar W. Maddaus (I'll reference him as Oscar W. or Oscar Wilhelm to differentiate him from his son Oscar who we usually referred to as Uncle Oscar. Oscar Wilhelm was also known in America as Oscar

William and had a son Oscar, Jr., as well--see below) was the second son of Johann Karl Ludwig and Adele Maddaus and the most adventurous. Born in 1845, he appears in Brooklyn in the late 1860s. His name does not show up on any ship passenger lists from that decade. He must have made at least 3 crossings from Riga to New York or New York to Riga.

The earliest evidence of Oscar W. Maddaus is found in Marriage Records for Kings County (Brooklyn), NY for August 2, 1868 marriage to Maggie Borwy (sic), age 18, daughter of Hugh Bowry and Jane Purber. The 1870 Census for the 22nd Ward of the city of Brooklyn, lists him as age 25 and a wood engraver of Russian heritage, due of course to the fact that his birthplace was Riga, located in the Russian Empire. The household includes Margaret, age 21, Oscar, Jr. age 1/12 and James Brown, an errand boy aged 15. Births of three children came in successive years of 1870 (Oscar, Jr.), 1871 (Adelaide) and 1872 (Clara Adele).

The Maddaus name next appears in the Brooklyn Eagle death notices, dated December 28, 1872, although it does not mention Oscar W. by name:

> MADDAUS---December 27, at 2 P.M., our little daughter, CLARA ADELE MADDAUS, at the age of 4 months and 14 days.
>
> Friends are invited to attend the funeral from the house 323 Twelfth street, South Brooklyn, Sunday, 29th at 3:30PM, the afflicted parents.

The following August 18, 1873 Brooklyn Eagle death notices include a longer listing as follows:

> MADDAUS--On the 16th of August, at 1 P. M., our dearly loved wife and sister, MARGARET MADDAUS, after two weeks' suffering, at the youthful age of 24 years, 4 months and 14 days.
>
> Having been so good and faithful a wife and mother, she sacrificed her own dear self to her nursing and comforting of her husband and little ones, whom she has gone to meet in Heaven. The funeral services will be held at 323 Twelfth street, South Brooklyn, at her late residence on Wednesday, the 20th, 11 A. M. Our friends, all of who loved her, are invited to attend by the broken-hearted

husband and brother. O. W. Maddaus and James Brown.

The family apparently fell victim to the 1872-3 influenza epidemic that impacted much of North America beginning in the Toronto area in 1872, with Margaret the last of the four to die. Oscar certainly had to be devastated and the notice has the voice of his brother-in-law James for good reason.

Burial records from the Green-Wood Cemetery in Brooklyn list Clara Adele Maddaus and her mother Margaret Maddaus, as well as Adelaide Maddaus and Oscar Maddaus, all with the same date of Interment of August 20, 1873, Lot 17245, Section 17. Dates of death for Adelaide and young Oscar are unknown.

For Oscar Wilhelm, the 5 years certainly brought many joys and the ultimate in heartbreak. He became naturalized in late 1873 and applied for a passport which was issued in June of 1875 but otherwise no public record. He is on one transatlantic passenger list in October 1875, from Bremen to New York, and the reason for the trip to the old country would arrive later: Augusta Rathminder agreed to marry him and follow him to America.

In addition to his first marriage and family, Oscar Wilhelm's early years in New York built his wood engraving business, and a number of examples of his engraving work are extant. Most of the examples relate to images created for commercial catalogs of the day, which pre-dated the use of photography. Two engravings appear in early 1870s in the "Illustrated Catalogue of Goods Manufactured in The Comb Department of The India Rubber Comb Company" of College Point, NY. The combs in question were among those products utilizing hard rubber under the early patents of Goodyear and Conrad Poppenhusen. Oscar W. contributed engravings of the company's corporate office and factory. Another example of intricate wood engravings of Remington Sewing Machine on 'plain table' and 'half cabinet' appear in the company's 1880 catalogue of products.

He also performed as a violinist in a number of events. One documented in the Brooklyn Eagle of January 16, 1877, was a "Mollenhauser

Classical Soiree" at the Atheneum. The Eagle notes "the few hundred ardent music lovers who braved the severe storm last evening had abundant recompense for their courageous venturing in the classical soiree," the third of four scheduled. Works of Lachner, Mendelssohn, Rubinstein and J.S. Bach were featured.

Reed & Barton became a significant engraving customer of Oscar Wilhelm's in the mid-1870s, and he was tapped to produce images of their silverware for their catalogue in 1877. In "Standard of Living: The Measure of the Middle Class in America," Marina Moskowitz outlines the relationship between the company and the artist producing images of the company's wares for promotional purposes:

> The artists responsible for creating these images worked at the intersection of design and marketing. For illustrations of specific wares, artists completed wood engravings of objects, which were then reproduced by means of electrotypography, an innovation of the 1850s. Producers of these engravings were different from the original designers, and usually had long-term relationships with the companies who used their services. These artists were responsible for the huge catalogues of electrotypes produced in the 1870s and 1880s; in addition to depicting wares, these books were valued for their own artistry and were a testament to the companies' overall attention to art and design.

Reed & Barton's main competitor, The Meriden Britannia Company, had engravers on staff, whereas R & B used outside providers such as Oscar Wilhelm Maddaus for the work. Reed & Barton would ship silverware or photos of it, from Taunton, Massachusetts to New York to have the work done, and their New York representative would send Oscar's work back to Taunton to be prepared for printing in Springfield. The logistics of this process contributed to later difficulties.

When Reed & Barton embarked on a new catalogue in 1877, they escalated their relationship with Oscar Wilhelm but soon he had difficulty turning around his finished product and the company began to be unhappy with the quality and some human figures he produced. One company memo indicated "Maddaus doesn't seem to excel at this," and a second engraver was hired to complete the work. By 1885, Reed and Barton had an engraver working on site in Taunton, ensuring faster turnaround for the work.

With engraving work for Reed & Barton causing difficulties and a new wife and daughter, Oscar Wilhelm had a decision to make. Augusta Dorothea Rathminder, arrived in late 1875 or early in 1876 and their marriage was followed by the birth of Elsa in May of 1877. I can only speculate, as no documentation exists to support it, but it may be that letters from Riga in summer or autumn of 1877 indicated that Johann Karl Ludwig Maddaus had resigned from his teaching position in July and was in poor health and the family had either explicitly asked the young couple to come back to Riga, or they felt obligated to.

The next spring, their second child was born--in Riga--and they would stay for just over 5 years. Between early 1878 and October of 1883, both Johann Maddaus (1878) and Jānis Rātminders (1880) would die, and Oscar (1878), Ingo (1879), Senta (1880), Frieda (1881) and Harold (1882) were born.

While back in Riga, wood engraving seemed to be secondary to a new and diverse importing business making use of contacts from America. In October of 1877, he advertised sale of a silverware and other items from a shop at Herrenstrasse 21. Later, from a shop at Smilsu iela 8, Oscar marketed tools for woodworking, and a number of other labor-saving contraptions manufactured in the US. He would produce engravings of the items and place classified ads in "Rigasche Zeitung," the daily newspaper. He also represented International Harvester in parts of the Russian Empire ranging east into Russia.

Whether it was the import/export trade or some other business, by 1882 Oscar Wilhelm planned a move back to Brooklyn and he departed ahead of his family in late 1882 or early 1883. Augusta and the 6 children followed in October of 1883, as I have described earlier. This would be their last crossing of the Atlantic. Only Augusta would ever see Riga or visit her family again, this on a 1912 trip with Ingo, Sr., Julia and three-year-old Ingo, Jr. as an extension of his business trip to Berlin.

Oscar Wilhelm's career from 1883 to his death was characterized by a number of failed schemes and a wild imagination. It's unclear whether he continued his wood engraving, importing or music, and he called himself an engineer in the 1890 census. The family lived on 16th Street just south of Prospect Park, and he must have generated income to support their lifestyle.

Oscar Wilhelm's vagaries included bringing suit against a Mr. Joseph Todd in City Court, New York, in 1885 for $790, the balance due on a $1,000 contract for "work performed for digging for hidden treasure in Long Island City." Todd countersued for $400 for monies sent on the contract and was successful in his countersuit.

In 1891, his proposition to Thomas Edison to supply a new form of lightbulb filament was met with a letter from Edison's office, basically indicating that her already had the material and would not require his services.

Probably his ultimate indignity came in August of 1892 when he was charged with assault in a rather bizarre incident. He had contacted the brokerage firm of Kant & Friede in the Columbia Building at 29 Broadway looking for investors for his plan to build a railway from Russia across the Bering Strait to Alaska. His appointment with the two partners proceeded with Oscar Wilhelm proposing to be 51 percent stockholder in the venture and offering a 49 percent share to investors that the firm would secure. No details of the proposal would make the news and likely he had little idea how to make it happen, although who knows? The conversation went south when he qualified the offer by indicating that he would exclude any investors of Jewish background. Kant took offence and a scuffle ensued in which the partner's leg was fractured. Maddaus was 'held for examination' in Tombs police court with the examination set for August 23, 1882, according to a short article in the Brooklyn Eagle newspaper. No further newspaper coverage reveals the outcome of the examination or any penalties or sentences. And no mention of the incident managed to be passed down to my generation of the family. No wonder!

Oscar Wilhelm's death is also somewhat of a mystery. The Brooklyn Eagle's death notices of September 18, 1896 indicate he died the previous day.

> MADDAUS--On Thursday, September 17, OSCAR W. MADDAUS, beloved husband and father, aged 51.
>
> Funeral services to take place at his late residence, 478 Sixteenth St. Sunday, September 20, at 4 P. M. Internment at convenience of family.

No cause of death is listed and no news articles mention his death, but one indication I had (I think from Aunt Freida, long ago) was that it was the result of an accident in the street. His life and accomplishments seemed to quickly fade in the family memory to the point where I heard very little if anything about him.

Chapter Twenty-One

The Beauty and Power of Latvian Music and The Latvian Song and Dance Festival, 2013

Music has been a large part of my life from the time when my parents show tunes and my eldest brother John's Kingston Trio and Peter, Paul and Mary played on vinyl records in our living room. Performing music began with my covert interest in my older brother Alan's Gibson archtop guitar. He would take lessons and aspired to be the next coming of Dwayne Eddy, who his music instructor said Alan could equal in skills in less than a year. I ultimately ended up with the Gibson and (sadly) graduated to an electric Hofner guitar in my earliest rock n roll stage. Many six strings followed along with other instruments of 12 and 8 strings throughout my lifetime.

It's not surprising then that various forms of Latvian music would interest me. I have followed the career of Astro'n'out and Māra Upmane-Holstein since meeting her father Eižens in 2009 and purchasing a Latvian music compilation CD came during one of my first trips. Our cousin Lelde sensed this early on and regularly sends me home with a recommendation, once a CD of a variety of tunes she ripped from her musical catalog and another time the gift of a CD by Raxtu Raxti, a thoroughly delightful Latvian group who performs music from a variety of Latvian folk sources in modern arrangements. Lelde has also recommended Elīna Garanča's opera music, having known her since they were teenagers in the same choral group.

I was familiar with "The Singing Revolution" video documenting Estonia's peaceful and lyrical drive for independence in the late 1980s and early 1990s and found the Latvian parallel singing (and dancing) tradition to be every bit as compelling. On our visit in 2011, Lelde mentioned we might enjoy the Latvian National Song and Dance Festival two years hence and we did our homework on what exactly was involved. We booked our hotel room as soon as the dates of the festival were announced.

Knowing both great, great grandfathers were in attendance in the first Latvian Song Festival in 1873 piqued my interest as well. Apparently, Jānis Rātminders had written lyrics for a song "In Our Power, In Our Efforts" for the dedication of the Riga Latvian Society and while the song didn't rise to popularity, others of that time did. Johann Maddaus was trying out his photography skills at the German Song Festival in Riga a few years before and conceivably both were at the 1873 event.

Tickets to the 2013 Song Festival were available online so on a March morning at 4:00 AM, I was up, though maybe not totally awake, awaiting the opening of the "Biļešu Paradīze" portal in hopes purchasing tickets. This is not that easy, I would find (later we had even more difficulty with the 2018 ticket purchases).

For the uninformed, the Song and Dance Festival takes place once every five years around the first week in July and the week long schedule of events touches virtually every form of song and dance from traditional folk songs to orchestral music. The finale is an evening of mostly choir music held in the Mezaparks concert venue outside Riga, surrounded by tall pines and with breezes coming in from the Sea and the neighboring lakes.

Our first event in 2013 was a folk music concert at the Kipsala Exposition Center featuring a number of performers tracing the development of the music from the dainas first sung in the fields to kokle (dulcimer-like lap instrument) music to more modern adaptations of the dainas. In addition to the unique sound of the kokles, we heard for the first time the contemporary 'postfolk' ensemble Iļģi, featuring vocalists Ilga Reizniece and Maris Muktupavels, and the dramatic bagpipes and drums of Auli. It was if our Latvian music compilation CD had come to life before our eyes! But so much more was yet to come.

I had bought tickets for the next night's Vocal Symphonic Music Concert at Arena Riga without any great expectations. I knew the tradition of classical music was also strong in Latvia but I was not prepared for the performance. No YouTube videos could quite capture the music and its intense emotional qualities Latvian composers from Andrejs Jurjāns to Alfrēds Kalniņš to Jāzeps Vītols to Pēteris Vasks and Raimonds Pauls were represented in the program, which had not only the characteristic Latvian dainas underscoring the musical themes, but the strength and musicianship of a 250 piece orchestra and choir of over 600 voices. Added to all this were outstanding solos by the likes of saxophonist Oskars Petrauskis, Egils Upatnieks on English horn and Accordionist Ksenija Sidorova, as well as a number of terrific vocalists.

As the program continued, I felt immersed in the music and the feelings it evoked, and during the performance of the Zigmars Liepiņš/Māra Zālīte composed 'Fragments from the rock-opera Bearslayer," the emotional connection reached a crescendo as orchestra and chorus repeated the refrain "Tas ir laiks" (It is the time). Knowing the Bearslayer legend and the 1988 rock-opera on which it was based, I sensed the overwhelming sense of destiny on the part of the Latvian people and their culture which had so long been trampled over by their more powerful neighbors. Fittingly the program concluded with Raimonds Pauls "To My Native Land," although I would learn this was bittersweet for the composer, as he was excluded from participation in the Final Concert later in the week.

For me, the two events we had seen would have been enough but we still had a Dance performance and the Final Concert to attend. To say we were immersed in the experience would be an understatement. For anyone who is Latvian or is interested in Latvian culture, this once every five years event is the opportunity to truly grasp what Latvia is about.

The Latvian Dance Grand Performance actually consists of two performances preceded by open rehearsals, in part to give the dancers who come from villages all over the country the opportunity to practice and perfect their routines and in part to allow enough opportunities for interested folks to enjoy the show. We met Lelde and Gatis at her Aunt Māra's and Uncle Voldemārs' apartment in Grīziņkalns, the neighborhood that also is the location of Daugava Stadium, the event venue. I wrote of this pre-event gathering in an earlier chapter, it was a unique event in itself.

Dance Performance at Daugava Stadium, 2013

"Tevu laipas" (Our Father's Piers) was the title of this mass folk-dancing program which presented the whole scope of Latvian folk-dancing going back to 1888, the first year it was added to the Song Festival. The music (pre-recorded for this event), the local costumes and the dance patterns and symbols all combine to give a kaleidoscope effect as dancers of every age weave in and out of the stadium. The physicality and symbolism are at once awe-inspiring.

> The XV Dance Celebration Grand Performance "Our father's pier" is intended as a story about Latvian wisdom. Values that make Latvians stronger as a nation are handed down from generation to generation -- work manners and customs, the power of the family hearth, respect one towards the other, love of the native land -- and are like bridges cast from the past into the future.
>
> The origins of dance are rooted in ritual, connected to the signs found on archaeological adornments and ethnographic costumes.

They are symbols of God, Laima, Māra, Thunder and other characters, symbols of our virtues, or existence and individuality.

Ancient signs live through the ages.

XV Dance Celebration Program

This is a national gathering with over 600 groups coming from every part of Latvia and representing every demographic element of the country. Groups of dancers varying from the final dance combines all 14,700 dancers in one choreographic climax. We were mesmerized throughout the performance and exhausted at the end, as if we had danced ourselves.

One more major performance, the Final Concert, awaits, but first we take a day in the country, to visit relatives in Vecpiebalga, returning in time to see Astro'n'out in concert at Kipsala.

We have tickets for the 'rehearsal' performance of the Final Concert on Saturday night in Mezaparks, again an extra complete dress rehearsal of the program to meet the demand for tickets. (The Sunday night Final is televised on LTV, so we are able to watch from our hotel room.)

Mezaparks provides a spiritual setting for the finale and once again we were met with performers in local costumes emanating from each and every town and village in the country. The official count is 431 choirs, including 26 diaspora choirs, 4 children's choirs and 12 guest choirs, along with 31 dance groups and 39 instrumental groups. In total over 15,700 voices are assembled.

The theme for 2013 is "Līgo!"

> Līgo* is a ritual of transformation, of spiritual and physical cleansing, fertility and, most importantly, one which sees the departure and return of the light (sunlight). Testimony to the fact that if we follow the rite of the solstice of nature, this revival is possible not only in the life of every individual, but also in that of an entire nation.

*Līgo is a refrain repeated in traditional Latvian 4-line verses sung at Midsummer, meaning "Let it thrive!"

XXV Latvian Song Festival Program

The program harkens to the first Latvian Song Celebration in Dikli, in 1864--9 years before the first official national festival and more than 5 decades until Latvia's independence--when four-part choirs gathered to honor their God and nation: "Let our hearts also rejoice today in common ritual of song and light!"

As in the performances earlier in the week, the music is representative of Latvian compositions from the earliest dainas to the contemporary works of the likes of Mārtiņš Brauns and Ēriks Ešenvalds. We know some of the songs from scanning YouTube and especially enjoy the Raimonds Tiguls/Nora Ikstena work "Dod, Dieviņi!" and the traditional folk-song "Put, vejini! (Blow, wind!) We have played and replayed previous performances of Brauns' "Saule, Pērkons, Daugava," which features lyrics from the poet Rainis, and when the full 17,000+ choir joins in to perform this song near the end of the performance, we're enraptured.

Mezaparks Final Concert Venue

One aspect I have not mentioned of the performances we saw, whether the Vocal Symphonic Concert or the Final Concert, is the reverence that Latvians hold for the conductors of each piece of music. Only the most highly regarded conductors are invited to participate.

Ojārs Ēriks Kalniņš, long-time Latvian diplomat and politician, perhaps said it best after the 2018 Final concert:

> Consider the conductor.
>
> He/she stands before 16,800 singers. Behind him are 40,000 more. And all, as one, respond to his commands. But they are not the commands a general or politician gives. He is more of a magician, who has learned the power of music and its emotional, spiritual and physical effect on the human soul. He has learned to master that power, its nuances and dynamics. Working with the equally magical power of the composer, the conductor channels that music through the hearts and minds of 56,000+ human beings, and they respond as one. Music is more than sound, it is the vibrations that enter the body and soul and performs complex biomechanical reactions within the human. There is a magic that occurs when one singer moves one listener. But multiply that by 50,000, and the effect is almost otherworldly.
>
> In Latvia, the real national heroes are those who have mastered the secrets and magical power of words and music: the poets, composers, musicians and conductors. Last night the ovations of 50,000 were directed to each and every one of them. And while all of us were moved by the music, imagine what it must feel like to be a conductor, in the midst of those 50,000, and to feel like the eye of a sublime musical hurricane. In Latvia, music is a deeply spiritual experience, and the conductor and composer are like ancient shamans who have unlocked the secrets of the universe and use them to bring joy to all around them.
>
> Ojārs Ēriks Kalniņš, Facebook post, July 9, 2018

The Song and Dance Festival provides that unique insight to the core of what Latvia and its people are all about, and while I know this type of tradition exists in other countries, I also know that Latvia's treasure is its song and dance tradition. We returned for the 2018 Festival with great anticipation and were not disappointed in the event as it coincided with the 100th Anniversary of Latvian independence. I know I will return every five years as long as I am able, the draw to this event is so strong.

In all my family research and the associated reading I have done, two books stand out as incredibly helpful in providing background for Latvian music:

> "The Power of Song: Nonviolent National Culture in the Baltic Singing Revolution" by Guntis Šmidchens
>
> "Song to Kill a Giant" by Sandra Kalniete

The former is probably the single most impressive work documenting the history of the Baltics through the understanding of the culture and music of Latvia, Estonia and Lithuania through the ages. The latter focuses more specifically on the efforts by Latvians, mirroring those of Estonians and Lithuanians, to break free of the Soviet hold on the Baltics. Neither is light reading and both are fascinating. If no others, I recommend these two

Šmidchens' book "aims to expand our knowledge of Baltic national cultures and nationalism...and contributes to our understanding of nonviolent political movements." He presents us with the early study of Baltic folk-songs by the 18th century philosopher Johann Gottfried Herder that leads us up to "The Singing Revolution" and the ever-present role that music plays in preserving and enriching the culture of the three Baltic countries.

Kalniete describes the role of song in the peaceful mass events, orchestrated as theatrical performances moving toward culmination. "The red-white-red flag and "God, Bless Latvia" had completely pushed the anthem out of our minds. The national prayer and flag belonged to us, the Latvian people, and we did not wish to share them -- something that would be inevitable if they were made official." She rejoices at the political culmination, "The USSR is gone! I could not absorb the enormity of this announcement. The evil empire was gone!" The power of song and its unifying force carried the Latvian people to freedom.

Surely no better example exists to support Oscar Wilde's assertion that "Life imitates art far more than art imitates life" than the music of Latvia. Whether the intricate choreographic patterns of the dance performance or the unity of voice in the songs, Latvians live their lives as a reflection of the ancient art from generations before arising from nature itself.

Chapter Twenty-Two

Latvia 100
A Year of Celebration, 2018

It was pre-ordained that we would return for the 2018 Latvian Song and Dance Festival and this would be a special celebration, not only for the Festival, but for the entire year. Latvia was to celebrate its 100th anniversary of the declaration of independence in 2018 ("Latvijas valsts simtgades"), with a calendar full of events extended throughout the year.

Tickets for the Festival became difficult to come by and I will skip the explanation of how we acquired them other than to say Beth was heroic in her internet monitoring skills and later we did resort to purchasing a few by somewhat covert means. The beginning of the Festival week found us housed in our favorite Monika Centrum Hotel suite overlooking Kronvalds Park and struggling once again with jetlag and the 7-hour time difference.

I also will not try to compare the 2013 Festival and the 2018 edition in general terms other than to say that both were outstanding. The programs varied, the events in and around Riga were plentiful and we thoroughly enjoyed every minute. We even took a couple days before to visit Kolka, Ventspils and Kuldiga in the wind and rain, giving Beth a chance to see the sites I had enjoyed on my visits there with relatives in prior years.

Winds and cool temperatures seemed to be the theme in terms of weather, unlike the usual July conditions in Riga, and that made for a challenge at outdoor evening events, especially the Dance Performance at Daugava Stadium and the Final Concert in Mezaparks. We saw a number of our relatives, connected with an Irish diaspora chorus which included a friend from one of my prior visits and made some new friends at the hotel, all sharing in our pleasure and awe at the week's events. We had a grand time and hated to have it end.

Looking back over some video highlights, I am still moved by the performances, especially the Final Concert's presentation of the Liepiņš/Zālīte "Fragments from rock-opera Bearslayer," this time featuring vocalist Dons (you know he's great because he is known by his given name only, like Cher or Elvis or Madonna), and a new composition by Raymonds Tiguls, "Lec, Saulite!," (Rise, Sun!) based on the old folk song. With over 16,000 voices, the music soars!

> Much more than a thousand points of light. The spark was lit in 1873. The light and the music shine on from generation to generation. Feeling the vibrations of 50,000 voices in harmony and unison is an experience unlike any other.
>
> Ojārs Ēriks Kalniņš, Facebook post, July 8, 2018

The Festival would not be my only visit, as I was determined to return for the National Holidays in November. And so, I booked my second flight. My goal: To experience both Lāčplēsis Day, November 11th, the day honoring soldiers who had fought for Latvian independence, and Proclamation Day of the Republic of Latvia, November 18th. I knew it would be special, and it was.

Torch Parade, 100th Anniversary of Proclamation of Latvian Independence

I participated in most of the events of the two holidays with great pleasure. It was the culmination, in a sense, of my understanding of Latvia as a culture and Latvia as a nation. Seeing the hundreds of candles lit by the wall of Riga Castle on Lāčplēsis Day, attending a special performance of Jāzeps Vītols Music School students at the Riga Latvian Society concert hall and marching with thousands of torch-bearing Latvians through the streets of Riga on the evening of Proclamation Day all served to validate my experience. While my Latvian language skills continue to fail me, I am able to sense the aura of the culture through osmosis or some other means, and I feel I understand.

Leaving Riga after the week of celebration, I flew to Helsinki for my Icelandair connection home to America, but this time I took advantage of Finland's early snow with a week of skiing in Vuokatti, a beautiful resort in central Finland. Skiing in the fading November light, I could not help but reflect on the week before, the decade of my discovery of Latvia and the years of family history I'd uncovered there.

The interconnectedness of all things in Latvian culture--nature, music, literature, dance, family--brings me back, year in year out. I am always amazed at how little the degrees of separation are--Riga at the center, but the hundreds of towns and villages and thousands of ancient farmsteads all spreading out like a tapestry, each thread connected and woven together to form one cohesive entity

The connections of family and country are similar. I noticed just a short time ago the relationship of the Latvian composer and musicologist Andrejs Jurjāns (1856-1922)--who's given us the Latvian Song Festival March and the beautifully haunting folk song "Put, Vejini" (Blow, wind), so revered by Latvians--to the Rātminders. Jurjāns was the nephew of Anna Ratmindere Jurjane, daughter of Andžs Rātminders and first cousin of Augusta Maddaus. Knowing this connection and his origin in Ergli, not far from Vecpiebalga, gives me a special sense of the music, beyond the melody and arrangement.

I reflected on the heritage as my father might have, through the numbers. Four of my 16 great, great grandparents lived most of their lives in Latvia; one, Jānis Rātminders was an active participant in the First Latvian Awakening of the mid-18th century. Both Rātminders literary and Maddaus artistic works are part of the early years of the Awakening and although they are now relegated to libraries, archives, museums and church altars, the nation was built on the works of those artists and their contemporaries.

On the 100th Anniversary of Proclamation Day of the Republic of Latvia, I joined the dignitaries and citizens of Latvia at the Freedom Monument and, lined-up by eights, flowers in hand, we approach the Monument in the Laying of Flowers ceremony. I am an American, but for a brief moment in time, the one quarter of my heritage that was part of Riga, the one-sixteenth of my ancestry that was truly Latvian, pulses in my blood and beats in my heart and, as I lay down the red and white and red flowers in my hands at the base of the Monument, I am Latvian in mind and spirit.

Appendix

Johann Karl Ludwig Maddaus Family

Johann Karl Ludwig Maddaus

    Born: Hamburg, February 21, 1820
    Baptized: St. Michaelis, Hamburg
    Married: Riga, December 12, 1842
    Died: Riga, August 1, 1878
    Buried: Lielie kapi (The Great Cemetery), Riga

Gertrud Adele Zirckmann Maddaus

    Born: Riga, September 9, 1823
    Baptized: Riga, October 15, 1823
    (Dorothea Adela Ernestine Gertrud Zirckmann)
    Died: Riga, December 8, 1908
    Buried: Lielie kapi (The Great Cemetery), Riga

Children:
1. Alexander Albert Maddaus

    Born: Riga, August 19, 1843
    Died: Riga, March 28, 1915
    Buried: Lielie kapi (The Great Cemetery), Riga

2. Oscar Wilhelm Maddaus

    Born: Riga, August 16/18, 1845
    Married: Margaret Brown
        Children:
    Married: Augusta Dorothea Rathminder

Children:
- Elsa, 1877
- Oscar, 1878
- Ingo, 1879
- Senta, 1880
- Frieda, 1881
- Ralph, 1882
- Ralph, 1890

Died: Brooklyn, NY, USA 1896
Buried: Green Wood Cemetery, Brooklyn

3. Ottilie Angelina Emilie Maddaus

Born: Riga, October 30, 1847
Died: Riga, May 20, 1913

4. Johanna Adele Maddaus

Born: Riga, May 8, 1850
Died: Riga, 1850

5. Johanna Elvira Maddaus

Born: Riga, October 14, 1851
Died: 1914

6. August Ludwig Maddaus

Born: Riga, February 6, 1854
Married: Ida Henriette Rickert, December 12, 1879 (died in childbirth)
Married: Wera Schurawoff
  Children:
    Adela Wera Maddaus
      Born: Riga, November 20, 1880
    Eugen Eduard Maddaus
      Born: Riga, September 2, 1882
    Arnna Gregor Maddaus
      Born: Riga, 1884
Died: Riga, November 21, 1897
Buried: Lielie kapi (The Great Cemetery, Riga)

7. Emma Gertrud Maddaus
>   Born: Riga, February 1857
>   Died: Riga, April 1860

8. Eugen Adolph Maddaus
>   Born: Riga, October, 1858
>   Died: Riga, April 1860

Johann Rathminder Family
(Jānis Rātminders)

Jānis Rātminders
>   Born: Vecpiebalga, December 8, 1812
>   Married: Riga, St. John's Church, September 22, 1846
>   Died: Riga, October 8, 1880
>   Buried: Martina kapi (St. Martin's Cemetery), Riga

Maria Louise Jacobsohn Rathminder
>   Born: Riga, December 1824
>   Died: Riga, January 29, 1909

Children:

1. Johann Heinrich Rathminder
>   Born: Riga, May 1847

2. Ida Amalie Rathminder
>   Born: Riga, July 1849

3. Augusta Dorothea Rathminder
> Born: Riga, 1850
> Died: Brooklyn, NY, 1937
> Buried: Green Wood Cemetery, Brooklyn, NY

4. Marie Juliane Rathminder
> Born: Riga, October, 1851
> Repatriated to Germany: 1941

5. Emma Charlotte Rathminder
> Born: Riga, June, 1853

6. Wilhelm Karl Rathminder
> Born: Riga, October 1854

7. Eugenie Antonie Rathminder (Tante Jenny)
> Born: Riga, May 1856
> Married: _____Freimanis
> Died: Riga, 1937

8. Louise Helene Rathminder
> Born: Riga, June 1858

9. Ella Clementine Rathminder
> Born: Riga, January 1861

10. Olga Constance Rathminder
> Born: Riga, March 1863

Resources

Krišjānis Barons, editor, *Latvian Songs. Latvian Folksongs. Interlinear translation*. Riga: Institute of Literature, Folklore and Art, University of Latvia, 2012.

Inguna Bauere, *Skolas Līze*. Riga: Zvaigzne ABC, 2011.

Inguna Bauere, *Vecpiebalga. Ieraudzit, Iepazit, Izjust (Vecpiebalga: To See, To Know, To Feel)*. Vecpiebalga, 2007.

Aija Braslina, compiler, *The Birth of Latvia, Art and Age: from de facto to de iure*. Riga: SIA Neputns, 2008.

Augusts Deglavs, *Riga, Book 1, Patriots*. Riga: Jumava SIA, 2017.

Daina Stukuls Eglitis, Imagining the Nation: History, Modernity, and Revolution in Latvia. University Park, PA: The Pennsylvania State University Press, 2002.

Modris Eksteins, *Walking Since Daybreak, A Story of Eastern Europe, World War II, and the Heart of Our Century*. New York: Houghton Mifflin Company, 1999.

Gustav Freytag, *Ingo, The Warriors Return*. New York: P. F. Collier & Son, 1901.

Thomas L. Friedman, *The World Is Flat: A Brief History of the Twenty-First Century*. New York: Farrar, Strauss and Giroux, 2005.

Uldis Gērmanis, *The Latvian Saga*. Riga: Atēna, 2007.

James E. Haas, *Conrad Poppenhusen: The Life of a German-American Industrial Pioneer*. Baltimore: The Gateway Press, 2004.

Sandra Kalniete, *With Dance Shoes in Siberian Snows*. Campaign and London: Dalkey Archive Press, 2001.

Andreas Kasekamp, *A History of the Baltic States*. New York: Palgrave

MacMillan, 2010.

Erik Kirschbaum, *Burning Beethoven, The Eradication of German Culture in the United States during World War I*. New York: Berlinica Publishing LLC, 2014.

Eduards Kļaviņš, Editor, *Art History of Latvia, Volume III, 1780-1890*. Riga: Institute of Art History of the Latvian Academy of Art; Art History Research Support Foundation, 2019.

Edward Connery Lathem, Editor, *The Poetry of Robert Frost*. New York: Henry Holt and Company, LLC, 1979.

W. Bruce Lincoln, *Nicholas I, Emperor and Autocrat of All the Russians*. DeKalb, Illinois: Northern Illinois University Press, 1989.

John E. Maddaus, *Maddaus Family History*. Orono, Maine, 1995.

Eileen Reid Marcil, *Our German Granny*. Charlesbourg, Quebec, 2005.

Vitolds Mašnovskis, *The Lutheran Churches of Latvia, Volume 1*. Riga: SIA DUE, 2005.

Vitolds Mašnovskis, *The Lutheran Churches of Latvia, Volume 2*. Riga: SIA DUE, 2006.

Vitolds Mašnovskis, *The Lutheran Churches of Latvia, Volume 3*. Riga: SIA DUE, 2007.

Vitolds Mašnovskis, *The Lutheran Churches of Latvia, Volume 4*. Riga: SIA DUE, 2007.

E. B. Matthews, Editor and Translator, *Twelve Poems by Kārlis Skalbe*, English Translations with Latvian Text (Stockholm: The Daugava Press, 1953). Philadelphia: 1996.

W. K. Matthews, translator and compiler, *A Century of Latvian Poetry*. London: John Calder Publishers, 1957.

Barry Moreno, *Castle Garden and Battery Park*. Charleston, SC: Arcadia Publishing, 2007.

Marina Moskowitz, *Standard of Living, The Measure of the Middle Class in Modern America*. Baltimore: Johns Hopkins University Press,

2004.

Valters Nollendorfs et. al. compilers, *The Three Occupations of Latvia, 1940-1991: Soviet and Nazi Take-Overs and Their Consequences*. Riga: Museum of the Occupation of Latvia, 2013.

Larry W. Phillips, Editor, *Ernest Hemingway on Writing*. New York: Touchstone, 1999.

Jānis Polis, *Vecpiebalga novada Inesu pagasts*. Aluksne: SAI SELJA, 2008.

Inta Pujāte, Dainis Bruģis, compilers, *Portrets Latvija 19.gadsimts (Portraits of 19th Century Latvia)*. Riga: SIA Neputns, 2014.

Andrejs Pumpers, *Bearslayer, The Latvian Legend*, Translated by Arthur Cropley. Riga: Latvian University Academic Publishing, 2007.

Edvard Radzinsky, *Alexander II, The Last Great Tsar*. New York: Free Press, 2005.

James Rebanks, The Shepherd's Life, Modern Dispatches from an Ancient Landscape. New York: Flatiron Books, 2016.

Jukka Rislakki, *The Case for Latvia, Disinformation Campaigns Against A Small Nation*. Leiden, Netherlands: Editions Rodopi B. V., 2014.

Christine Sleeter, *White Bread, Weaving Cultural Past into the Present*. Rotterdam: Sense Publishers, 2015.

Guntis Šmidchens, The Power of Song, Nonviolent National Culture in the Baltic Singing Revolution. Seattle: University of Washington Press, 2014.

Arturs Snips, *Klejojumi*. Riga: Communication Management and Consulting, 2010.

Timothy Snyder, *Bloodlands: Europe Between Hitler and Stalin*. New York: Basic Books, 2010.

Fritz Stern, Five Germanys I Have Known. New York: Farrar, Strauss and Giroux, 2006.

Arveds Schwabe, *The Story of Latvia, A Historical Survey*. Stockholm: E. Olofssons Boktryckeri AB, 1949.

Kārlis Skalbe, *Dzejas Izlase* (A Selection of Poetry). Riga: Zvaigzne ABC, 2005(?).

James & Maureen Tusty et al., *The Singing Revolution*. DVD, 2006.

Ieva Zauberga et al., Eds., *Bear's Ears: An Anthology of Latvian Literature*. Yliopistopaino: Helsinki University Press, 1997.

Vita Zelče, *Latviešu avīžniecība: laikraksti savā laikmetā un sabiedrībā, 1822-1865* (Latvian Newspapers in the Context of Their Times, 1822-1865). Riga: Zinātne Publishers, 2009.

About the Author

Charles L. "Charlie" Maddaus was born in Schenectady, NY and grew up in the Capital District of Upstate New York. Upon graduation from Scotia-Glenville High School, he pursued a degree in English from Bates College in Lewiston, Maine, and settled in Northern New England. Careers in resort management, music, and banking led to a career in teaching high school English in schools in Maine, Vermont and New Zealand. He retired to Oxford County in Western Maine, and continues to write, read, play guitar, run, Nordic ski and travel to Latvia, whenever he can.

www.ingramcontent.com/pod-product-compliance
Lightning Source LLC
Chambersburg PA
CBHW040251090526
44586CB00041B/2753